NHS
Digital

National Clinical Coding Standards OPCS-4

Accurate data for quality information

Produced by	Terminology and Classifications Delivery Service NHS Digital Vantage House 40 Aire Street Leeds LS1 4HT Information.standards@nhs.net
Website	http://systems.digital.nhs.uk/data/clinicalcoding
Date of issue	April 2018

✦ tso
part of Williams Lea Tag

Published by TSO (The Stationery Office), part of Williams Lea Tag,
and available from:

Online
www.tsoshop.co.uk

Mail, Telephone, Fax & E-mail
TSO
PO Box 29, Norwich, NR3 1GN
Telephone orders/General enquiries: 0333 202 5070
Fax orders: 0333 202 5080
E-mail: customer.services@tso.co.uk
Textphone 0333 202 5077

TSO@Blackwell and other Accredited Agents

First published 2018
First impression 2018

ISBN 9780113230730

Printed in the United Kingdom for The Stationery Office.
J003452856 c4 07/18

OPCS-4 CONTENTS

INTRODUCTION

The OPCS Classification of Interventions and Procedures (OPCS-4) is a statistical classification of interventions and procedures undertaken in the National Health Service (NHS) reflecting current clinical practice. OPCS-4 is an approved NHS Fundamental Information Standard.

The use of OPCS-4 assumes that:

- A patient health record (a medico-legal document) exists, and therefore it is meaningful to have codes that depend on what activity has been specified in that record.

- The record is translated and coded, applying the rules, conventions and national standards of the classification, by appropriately trained and qualified clinical coding staff.

- Existing data flows are also in place so that when the record is translated and coded, the data can flow from hospital Patient Administration Systems (PAS) and onwards to support local and national data requirements through the Secondary Uses Services (SUS).

The classification is mandatory for use by Health Care Providers to support various forms of data collections, such as Central Returns and Commissioning Data Sets (CDS). All Consultant Episodes (hospital provider) containing procedures must be recorded and collected using OPCS-4. The requirements for data sets and related definitions are specified in the NHS Data Model and Data Dictionary.

The statistical classification also supports various forms of secondary uses of information essential for planning and improving patient care. Among these secondary uses are:

- Operational and strategic planning,

- Resource use,

- National and local planning and performance management,

- Research and epidemiology,

- Department of Health initiatives, and

- NHS payment system.

OPCS-4 is used by NHS suppliers to build or update software to support NHS business functions and interoperability.

Background

A statistical classification of surgical operations has been available for use in the United Kingdom (UK) since 1944 when the Medical Research Council published one which identified 442 categories of operation. The then General Register Office prepared and issued an updated version in 1950, and revisions to this were subsequently issued in 1956, (first revision), 1969 (second revision) and 1975 (third revision).

This first classification contained 664 un-subdivided three-character categories. It was revised in 1956 with the addition of 10 categories, and again in 1969 at which time the three-character categories were increased to 731. Some of these categories were subdivided (extended to four-character subcategories) so that the classification contained 1183 valid codes. The third revision, in 1975, further expanded the classification to 1426 valid codes.

The fourth revision of the OPCS-4 was conceived in 1983 as a result of one of the recommendations in the first report in 1982 of the Steering Group on Health Services Information (SGHSI), chaired by Mrs E Korner.

The SGHSI recommended that, "as a matter of urgency, OPCS should provide operation codes, which reflect current clinical practice and develop procedures for the frequent updating of the classification".

The fourth revision of OPCS was initially issued in 1987 with definitive publication and implementation in 1990. The general objectives of the revision process, which began in 1983, were:

1. To identify and classify current surgical operations with particular reference to the incorporation of recent innovative techniques.

2. To eliminate rarely performed operations but to include procedures not requiring the full operating theatre environment.

3. To provide a flexible classification, responsive to less defined specialty boundaries and capable of future expansion.

Both the Tabular List and Alphabetical Index were updated in January 1990 and the Alphabetical Index was again revised in April 1993. OPCS-4 then contained 1183 three-character categories all of which were subdivided resulting in over 4000 valid codes.

It was originally devised as an instrument to provide the best possible basis for accommodating current systems and future developments for data on surgical operations. As well as maintaining the planned objective, the fourth revision also incorporated two further general aspects. It provided a definition of an operative procedure and outlined the concept of MAIN operation during an episode of care.

From 1995 a review of OPCS-4 was completed consulting with users to identify future need and inform future strategic direction.

In 2002 a project to develop an up to date intervention classification was commissioned by the Information Policy Unit (IPU). A proposal on behalf of the former NHS Information Authority and the IPU to produce a requirement for the development of a new classification was considered by the Information Standards Board on 19 April 2002 who then submitted their recommendations to Sir John Pattison and the National Information Policy Board (NIPB) for their approval. On 4 July 2002 the NIPB approved the proposal for this work to go ahead.

The former NHS Information Authority initiated the project to deliver a new intervention classification to replace OPCS-4.2 to support the DH Financial Flows project known as Payment by Results. A review of this project was undertaken in March 2005 with the migration of the project to NHS Connecting for Health on 1 April 2005. The decision was taken at this stage to develop and enhance OPCS-4.2 to meet the needs of the Payment by Results programme which relies on detailed and accurate coding.

Consequently, OPCS-4.2 was enhanced during 2005–6 to support delivery of an updated classification for implementation across the NHS from April 2006. The project was completed in close collaboration with the Department of Health and with the NHS Information Centre for health and social care (IC) revising Healthcare Resource Groups (HRGs). In addition, input was received from clinical members of the clinical Expert Working Groups co-ordinated by the IC, which represented the Royal Colleges and professional associations. The result was OPCS-4.3, reflecting changes in clinical care in recent years enabling clinicians, in cooperation with clinical coders, to better describe patient care information. As a result this improved the quality of clinical procedural data collected by the NHS.

At the end of the project the responsibility for the development and maintenance of the OPCS-4 classifications was transferred to the NHS Connecting for Health national Clinical Classifications Service, now known as the Terminology and Classification Delivery Service.

Since September 2007, the Terminology and Classifications Delivery Service has made it easier for stakeholders to provide requests for change and track their progress with the launch of the online OPCS-4 Requests Portal. This was designed so anyone could submit their suggestions whenever it suited them.

The OPCS-4.5 release of the classification was the first which included requests for change received through the portal from stakeholders of the NHS. The OPCS-4 Requests Portal continues to provide the mechanism for all stakeholders to submit their requests for change. https://isd.hscic.gov.uk/rsp/

The development and maintenance of the classification is undertaken by the Terminology and Classifications Delivery Service at NHS Digital and will continue until further notice.

Clinical coding

Clinical coding is the translation of medical terminology that describes a patient's complaint, problem, diagnosis, treatment or other reason for seeking medical attention into codes that can then be easily tabulated, aggregated and sorted for statistical analysis in an efficient and meaningful manner.

Clinical coder

A clinical coder is the health informatics professional that undertakes the translation of the medical terminology in a patient's medical record into classification codes. A clinical coder will be accredited (or working towards accreditation) in this specialist field to meet a minimum standard. Clinical coders use their skills, knowledge and experience to assign codes accurately and consistently in accordance with the classification and national clinical coding standards. They provide classification expertise to inform coder/ doctor dialogue. Clinical coders must abide by local and national confidentiality policies and codes of practice as a breach may lead to disciplinary action, a fine or, in the case of a breach of the Gender Recognition Act 2004, possible prosecution.

Hospital provider spell and consultant episode

A clinical coder must assign OPCS-4 codes to the procedures recorded in the medical record for each consultant episode (hospital provider) within the hospital provider spell for the Admitted Patient Care (APC) Commissioning Data Set (which includes day cases).

A hospital provider spell may contain a number of consultant episodes (hospital provider)[1] and the definitions for these terms are found in the NHS Data Model and Dictionary at: http://www.datadictionary.nhs.uk/

The NHS Data Model and Dictionary is the source for assured information standards to support health care activities within the NHS in England. It is aimed at everyone who is actively involved in the collection of data and the management of information in the NHS.

The concept of a finished consultant episode, commonly abbreviated to "FCE" is widely used in the NHS and has been used in previous clinical coding guidance.

See the NHS Data Model and Dictionary frequently asked questions for more information at: http://systems.digital.nhs.uk/data/nhsdmds/faqs

---

1 Consultant episode (hospital provider) is hereafter referred to as consultant episode.

DATA QUALITY

Medical record

A health record is defined in the Data Protection Act 1998 as a record consisting of information about the physical or mental health or condition of an individual made by or on behalf of a health professional in connection with the care of that individual. The health record can be held partially or wholly electronically or on paper.

The health record (commonly referred to as the medical record and used hereafter) is the source documentation for the purposes of clinical coding. The responsible consultant, or healthcare practitioner, is accountable for the clinical information they provide. It must accurately reflect the patient's encounter with the health care provider at a given time.

The clinical coder expects to find all relevant clinical information in the medical record and attributed to the relevant consultant episode within the hospital provider spell.

The structure and contents of the medical record may vary from hospital to hospital. Typically there are handwritten notes, computerised records, correspondence between health professionals, discharge letters, clinical work-sheets and discharge forms, nursing care pathways and diagnostic test reports. Any of these sources may be accessed for coding purposes. The accuracy, completeness and legibility of the medical record are critical to the assignment of the correct OPCS-4 code(s) and the production of robust health care information.

When the medical record does not contain sufficient information to assign a code, the clinical coder must consult the responsible consultant (or their designated representative[2]).

The clinical coder (or manager) should use the local information governance and clinical governance arrangements to address documentation issues and support data quality improvements.

The national clinical coding standards cannot provide direction to compensate for deficiencies in the documentation or coding process.

Information on standards for professional record keeping, developed by the Royal College of Physicians Health Informatics Unit and approved by the Academy of Medical Royal Colleges, can be found on the Royal College of Physicians website at.
https://www.rcplondon.ac.uk/resources/standards-clinical-structure-and-content-patient-records

Information governance and clinical governance

The lack of information, or discrepancies, in the medical record should be addressed through local information governance and clinical governance mechanisms. Such instances present an opportunity to lever change which will bring benefits to the organisation: such as improved recording of clinical information, robust local processes and correctly coded clinical data.

It is acceptable to agree local coding policy, provided this does not contravene any national coding standard.

When agreement has been reached through local governance on how to address a documentation or recording issue, the outcome must be documented in the departmental policy and procedure document. This must be agreed and signed-off by the clinical director and/or governance authority dependent on local arrangements. Local coding policies should be reviewed regularly as part of the organisation's review process.

Further information on information governance can be found at: http://systems.digital.nhs.uk/infogov

---

2 Hereafter referred to as the responsible consultant. The designated representative could be the clerking doctor, midwife or specialist nurse. As there will be local variations in designated representatives and processes the coding manager should confirm with the medical director the role of designated representative(s) in each specialty and document in the organisation's clinical coding policy and procedures document.

Clinical coding audit

Coded clinical data are audited against national clinical coding standards. Clinical coding audit must be objective and provide value to the local organisation by highlighting and promoting the benefits of taking remedial actions to improve data quality and processes as well as acknowledging evidence of best practice.

When there are documentation discrepancies or recurring reporting issues which are outside the remit or control of the clinical coding department, the audit report should highlight these to be addressed through the local information governance and clinical governance arrangements.

Local coding policy and procedure documents should be inspected as part of a clinical coding audit to ensure these:

- are up-to-date

- evidence local agreements and implementation

- have been applied consistently

- do not contravene national clinical coding standards.

Terminology to OPCS-4 cross-maps

Health care providers that have implemented electronic health records and a clinical terminology such as SNOMED CT use linkages between the terminology and OPCS-4 known as 'cross-maps' to enable the clinical coding of electronic health records.

These cross-maps are semi-automated with default and, where appropriate, alternative OPCS-4 target codes are provided. The default OPCS-4 target codes are acceptable for the terminology concept/term to which they are linked. However where there is more relevant detail within the record, the selection of alternative OPCS-4 target codes may need to be undertaken to ensure national clinical coding standards are consistently applied.

The national cross-maps are compliant with clinical coding national standards. They are provided in the NHS Digital UK SNOMED CT Clinical Edition biannual releases. They are designed to support those organisations with electronic health systems to fulfil the mandatory requirement for collection and reporting of intervention and procedure data using the NHS Information Standard, OPCS-4.

The classification cross-maps are compiled by the Terminology and Classifications Delivery Service to reflect the rules and conventions of OPCS-4 as well as the national clinical coding standards contained in this standards' reference book.

The cross-maps are available for download via the Technology Reference Data Update Distribution (TRUD) service following registration at the following website: https://isd.hscic.gov.uk/trud3/user/guest/group/0/home

Coding Uniformity

Uniformity means that whenever a given procedure performed during a consultant episode is coded, the same code(s) is always used to represent that procedure. Uniformity is essential if the information is to be useful and comparable.

General rules for accurate selection of codes apply:

- Code the minimum number of codes which accurately reflect the patient's interventions/procedure(s) performed during the consultant episode.

- Code each procedure to the furthest level of specificity, i.e. fourth character, which is available in the classification and supported by the medical record.

Three dimensions of coding accuracy

- **Individual codes**

  Each procedure should have the correct code assignment. An individual patient may have many procedures.

- **Totality of codes**

  The concept of totality of codes is complex. It means that all codes necessary to give an accurate clinical picture of the patient's procedures performed during a consultant episode encounter, must be assigned in accordance with the rules, conventions and standards of the classification. This is important as it is possible for a list of codes to describe a procedure incorrectly in terms of clinical coding rules and standards even though the individual codes selected are correct.

- **Sequencing of codes**

  Codes must be sequenced in accordance with clinical coding standards to provide consistent data for statistical analysis. A significant aspect of sequencing is the selection of main procedure. ***See PRule 2: Single procedure analysis and multiple coding.***

The four step coding process

The four staged process that make up the act of coding is designed to ensure appropriate and consistent code assignments. The coder is required to use OPCS-4 Volume II, Alphabetical Index and Volume I, Tabular List and be trained in the use of OPCS-4 and the context in which it is used.

The four step coding process is the key to ensuring correct use of OPCS-4 and accurate coding of the procedural statement(s) in the medical record. An overview of the four steps is provided below as a reminder. The full detail of each step is fully explored in training using national core curriculum training materials.

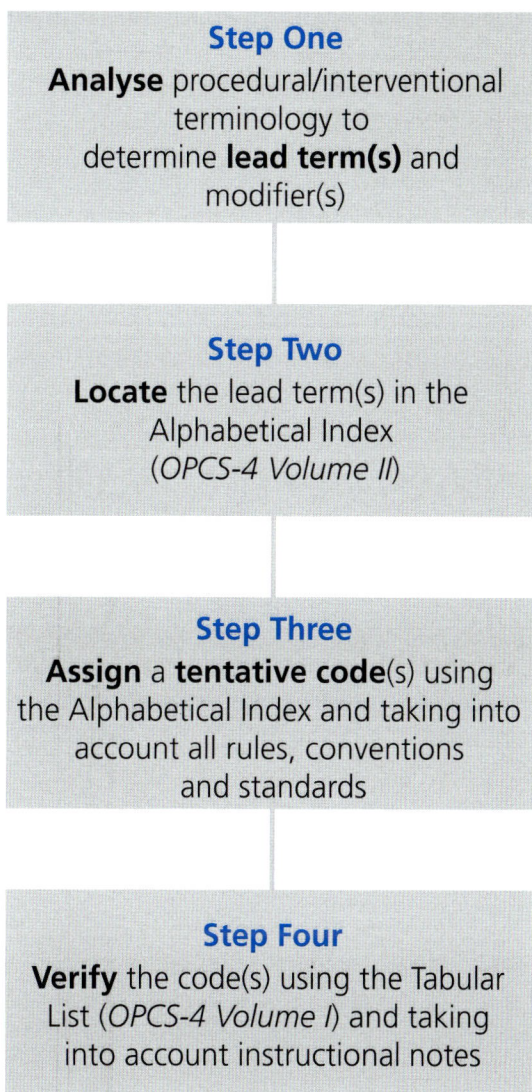

Step One
Analyse procedural/interventional terminology to determine **lead term(s)** and modifier(s)

Step Two
Locate the lead term(s) in the Alphabetical Index (*OPCS-4 Volume II*)

Step Three
Assign a **tentative code**(s) using the Alphabetical Index and taking into account all rules, conventions and standards

Step Four
Verify the code(s) using the Tabular List (*OPCS-4 Volume I*) and taking into account instructional notes

NATIONAL CLINICAL CODING STANDARDS OPCS-4 REFERENCE BOOK

The national clinical coding standards provide a reference source primarily aimed at clinical coders. The level of detail reflects the assumption that users will be trained in the use of the OPCS-4 classification as well as the abstraction of relevant information from the medical record.

Authorised amendments to the reference book are compiled and issued only by NHS Digital – Terminology and Classifications Delivery Service.

This reference book of national clinical coding standards is an evolving product and builds on the previously issued OPCS-4 Clinical Coding Instruction Manual. As the main emphasis of clinical coding is data quality and accuracy this reference book will focus on the clinical coding standards that must be applied when assigning OPCS-4 codes.

It is important that coders possess knowledge of the anatomy of the human body and that they are aware of the methods and processes used when a procedure/intervention is performed on a patient. Therefore a separate reference document containing supplementary information about more complex or less well known procedures accompanies this reference book. There is a host of reference sources available to coders if they wish to find out how a procedure is performed, such as surgical text books, the internet and of course the wealth of knowledge that exists within clinical staff at Trusts. The OPCS-4.8 Supplementary Information can be downloaded from the Main Publications page on Delen.

Structure of the OPCS-4 reference book

This reference book is split into distinct sections so that it is clear whether the rule, convention or standard must be applied throughout the classification, or if it should be applied throughout a chapter or if it is specific to a code(s) or procedure.

All rules, conventions and standards within the reference book have a unique identifier (reference number) and title so that they can be easily identified, applied and referenced, and they can be logically and consistently updated, removed or replaced. The reference numbers are specific to each section of the reference book, as explained below, but all are preceded by the letter 'P' for 'procedure' to indicate that the rule, convention or standard is applicable to OPCS-4.

Where there is no section for a chapter this means there are no standards or guidance specific to the chapter, e.g. Chapter F Mouth.

It is important that users understand how each section of the reference book should be applied when coding.

Rules of the OPCS-4

Rules of the OPCS-4 apply throughout the classification and the clinical coder must be aware of these rules in order to code with consistency and accuracy.

A rule that a coder must comply with is presented in a grey box. Explanatory information about the rule is presented in a white box.

The unique identifiers for rules begin with '**PRule**', and are followed by the number of the rule and the title (e.g. **PRule 7: Subsidiary Chapters Y and Z**).

Conventions of the OPCS-4

Conventions of the OPCS-4 are fundamental to accurate coding and apply throughout the classification (including the Alphabetical Index). The clinical coder must thoroughly understand these conventions and always apply them to ensure correct code assignment and sequencing.

Conventions of the OPCS-4 are presented within a grey box.

The unique identifiers for conventions begin with '**PConvention**' followed by the number of the convention and the title (e.g. **PConvention 2: Instructional notes and paired codes**).

Coding Standards

A Coding Standard must be applied by the clinical coder in the manner described. Compliance with a coding standard enables consistent, accurate and uniform coding which in turn supports the collection and comparison of local and national data across time. Standards are clear, concise and unambiguous.

Each standard is contained within a grey box. They may also have associated guidance and this will be contained within an adjoining white box. **Only the text within the grey area is the coding standard** e.g.

PGCS6: Radical operations

When coding radical operations:

- Code assignment must fully reflect the procedure(s) performed during the radical operation

- Instructional **Notes** must be applied in order to fully reflect all procedures performed

- Any uncertainty as to what procedures were performed during the radical operation must be clarified with the responsible consultant in order to ensure correct code assignment.

Radical operations generally involve procedures on multiple sites. This may include the removal of blood supply, lymph nodes and adjacent structures of a diseased organ and is often used in the treatment of malignant neoplasms.

Radical operations are generally not listed in the Alphabetical index or the Tabular list of OPCS-4.

There are three types of Standard:

- **General coding standards**

  General coding standards are located at the beginning of the reference book and applicable throughout the classification.

  The unique identifiers for general coding standards begin with '**PGCS**' followed by the number of the standard and the title (e.g. **PGCS2: Diagnostic versus therapeutic procedures**).

- **Chapter standards**

  Chapter standards are located at the beginning of each OPCS-4 chapter of the reference book and are applicable throughout the chapter.

  The unique identifiers for chapter standards begin with '**PChS**' followed by the chapter letter, the number of the standard and the title (e.g. **PChSL3: Insertion of stents and stent grafts**).

- **Coding standards**

  Coding standards are located throughout each OPCS-4 chapter of the reference book and applicable to specific procedures/interventions, codes, categories or blocks of codes. Coding standards are, generally, listed in code, category or range order.

  The unique identifiers for coding standards begin with '**PCS**' followed by the chapter letter, the number of the standard and the title (e.g. **PCSA1: Guide tube anterior cingulotomy (A03.1)**).

Coding guidance

Coding guidance is advice or information to aid the clinical coder or user of the classification. It does not describe a precise requirement or coding standard.

Coding guidance is contained within a white box. They do not have reference numbers or titles. e.g.

> Pessaries inserted into the vagina for antiseptic, contraceptive or abortifacient purposes are coded to Chapter Q.

Examples

Examples are included throughout the reference book to illustrate the correct application of a rule, convention or standard and are provided after guidance to illustrate the points made. They are only included when an example of the practical application of codes may aid the coder in understanding the rule, convention or standard. The codes reflect the procedural statement given within the example. Where required a rationale is provided.

Examples are not national standards and should only be used as an aid to coding. Clinical coding must always be based on the information contained within the rule, convention or standard.

Further examples of how standards can be applied can be found in the current ICD-10 and OPCS-4 Exercise and Answer Booklets. These are available to anyone on request via information.standards@nhs.net.

References

References direct the user to a pertinent standard or guidance elsewhere in the reference book. A Reference has a title but does not have a unique identifier.

The Reference details the unique identifier and title of the relevant standard to aid user navigation. If directing to a standard the Reference is shown in a grey box. If the box is not grey then the reference directs to guidance.

The coder must navigate to and review the full standard that has been referenced in order to ensure correct understanding and application. E.g.

> **Parathyroid washout (B16.4)**
>
> **B16.4 Parathyroid washout** is a nuclear medicine imaging procedure and a code from categories **Y93, Y94, Y97** and **Y98** must not be assigned in addition.
>
> *See PCSU3: Nuclear medicine imaging procedures.*

Index of standards

The Index of standards lists all rules, conventions, general coding standards, chapter standards and coding guidance in the order they appear in the reference book. It can be used to locate a specific standard in the reference book.

Summary of Changes

The summary of changes lists each change that has been made between the previous and current release of the reference book in the order that they appear in the reference book.

Updating the reference book

Updated releases of the reference book may contain new or updated rules, conventions, standards and guidance. Existing content in the previous release of the reference book may have been deleted. In each case the updates are made in a consistent manner and are identified in the summary of changes. Users can also refer back to previous reference books to see how the standard and codes were applied historically.

New Rules, Conventions and Standards

A new rule, convention, general coding standard and chapter standard is added at the end of the relevant section with a new unique identifier and title.

A new coding standard within a chapter is added in code, category or range order to reflect the location of the code(s) that the standard applies to in the OPCS-4 Tabular List. The new entry is given a new unique identifier and title. This means that the unique identifiers for coding standards within a chapter may not always be listed sequentially.

The unique identifiers and title of all new entries can be referenced in the Index of standards.

Updated rules, conventions and standards

When a rule, convention or standard is updated, the necessary changes are made to the existing text and the unique identifier remains the same.

Deleted Rules, Conventions and Standards

A rule, convention or standard is deleted when it is no longer to be applied or has been superseded. Deleted entries are removed from the reference book.

New, updated and deleted guidance and references

New guidance and references are added in the most relevant location. They are deleted if no longer required. Guidance and references are updated by making the appropriate changes to the existing text of the guidance or reference.

RULES OF OPCS-4

PRule 1: Definition of an intervention

Interventions are those aspects of clinical care carried out on patients undergoing treatment:

- for the prevention, diagnosis, care or relief of disease;
- for the correction of deformity or deficit, including those performed for cosmetic reasons; and
- associated with pregnancy, childbirth or contraceptive or procreative management.

Typically this will be:

- surgical in nature; and/or
- carries a procedural risk; and/or
- carries an anaesthetic risk; and/or
- requires specialist training; and/or
- requires special facilities or equipment only available in an acute care setting.

PRule 2: Single procedure analysis and multiple coding

When a series of operations are recorded, it is traditional, as with diagnostic information, to select the first mentioned for routine analysis.

When classifying diagnostic information, the International Classification of Diseases and Health Related Problems (ICD) recommend criteria for the selection of the MAIN condition for single-cause analysis. OPCS-4 follows this precedent in that the intervention selected for single procedure analysis from records of episodes of hospital care should be the MAIN intervention or procedure carried out during the relevant episode which may not always be the first procedure performed during the consultant episode.

Multiple interventions are often carried out simultaneously. In OPCS-4 some combinations have been encompassed within a single category whilst others, with a seemingly similar relationship, are required to be coded separately. It is important that users of the classification adhere to the instruction notes provided within it to ensure correct selection and sequencing of the codes, **see PConvention 2: Instructional notes and paired codes.**

PRule 3: Axis of the classification

There are 24 chapters in total within the OPCS-4 classification. These comprise 20 chapters covering individual body systems (Chapters A–T and V–W), one for diagnostic imaging, testing and rehabilitation procedures (Chapter U) and one for miscellaneous procedures and operations covering multiple systems, e.g. transfusion, resuscitation (Chapter X). There are also two additional chapters providing subsidiary classifications, one for methods of operation (Chapter Y) and the other for sites and laterality of operation (Chapter Z).

The main axis of the classification is body system. Within any particular body system the axis is the organ and within any particular organ the axis is the specific operation/intervention. The operations/interventions are broadly listed in descending order of complexity, e.g. removal, then repair, then aspiration or manipulation, and are generally sequenced in a way which reflects their comparative significance in terms of resource use.

PRule 3: *continued*

The following guidelines help to identify the level of complexity:

Major	–	Total removal
		Functional replacement
		Transplant
Intermediate	–	Partial removal
		Partial destruction
		Reconstruction
		Repair
Minor	–	Biopsy
		Incision
		Aspiration
Non-operative procedures	–	Injection
		Examination
		Scan/Imaging
		Screening

In some chapters this major-minor hierarchy principle is either not applicable or not as evident as it should be due to the capacity issues described in *PRule 5: Capacity, overflow categories and principal and extended categories.*

PRule 4: Category and code structure

Code assignment must always be made to four character level to make the code valid.

The three character category code structure is a three-digit code with an alphabetic character in the first position followed by two numbers. Each three character category is subdivided with four-character codes (subcategories).

The four character code structure is a four-digit code with an alphabetic character in the first position followed by three numbers, with a decimal point before the third number. Four character codes sit within three character categories.

Each four character code identifies a specific method or approach for performing the procedure/intervention mentioned in the three character category title.

Each category is presented in a similar format, and usually includes the provision of a residual subcategory, 'Other specified' **.8**, and an 'Unspecified' **.9** subcategory.

The use of the residual subcategory **.8** follows the axis of the classification within the category and is used when the procedural method to be coded has been specified but is not classified at any of the other four character codes within the category.

For example; for the three character category **C47 Closure of cornea**, the residual subcategory is **C47.8 Other specified closure of cornea** and is assigned for a specified procedural method describing closure of cornea that is not described as a 'Suture', 'Adjustment to suture', 'Removal of suture', or 'Gluing'.

PRule 4: *continued*

The use of the unspecified subcategory **.9** also follows the axis of the classification within the category and is used when the procedural method to be coded has not been specified and therefore not enough detail has been provided to use any of the other codes (**.1** to **.8**) within the category.

For example; if the procedural method is not specified, and the documentation simply reads 'Closure of Cornea', code **C47.9 Unspecified closure of cornea** would be assigned.

PRule 5: Capacity, overflow categories and principal and extended categories

In order to maintain the structure of the classification **.8** and **.9** codes are available in both principal and the extended categories. Only the **.8** and **.9** codes in the principal category can be used. The **.8** and **.9** codes from the extended category must not be used.

The continual revision process naturally introduces some capacity issues as the classification expands.

As a result previous hierarchical body system structure may not be as evident when using OPCS-4. It is therefore imperative that strict use of the Alphabetical Index and Tabular List notes are made when assigning codes.

Where capacity issues arise, the following guidelines are followed:

New three-character categories are placed within chapter ranges, and four-character codes are added to existing categories where space allows. Alternatively, new codes are placed at the end of the specific body system chapter. For example, categories **H01** to **H03** are operations on the appendix, whereas category **H04** relates to operations on the colon and rectum. Therefore, if there is a requirement for a specific operation on the appendix to be included in OPCS-4, and no room exists within the categories **H01–H03**, yet space is available at the end of a chapter, the new code is sited there.

Overflow categories

When additional operations/interventions are required to be classified to that chapter but the chapter is full; overflow categories are created at the end of the chapter. Overflow categories take the same structure as other categories within OPCS-4 but they are assigned the letter O, no matter which chapter they are classified within.

Overflow categories can be found at the end of Chapters L Arteries and Veins, W Other Bones and Joints and Chapter Z Subsidiary Classification of Sites of Operation. Codes created in this way still form part of an existing chapter even though they have a different alpha prefix to the rest of the codes within the chapter.

Within the Alphabetical Index codes classified within overflow categories are identified by placing the letter of the chapter the overflow category is contained within in brackets at the end of the index entry, for example **O28.1 Artery Basilar site (Z)**.

PRule 5: *continued*

Principal and extended categories

There are instances where an existing category is full but additional procedures need to be classified to that category. This is achieved by creating an 'extended category', the category that requires extension becomes a 'principal category'. Navigation is achieved by the inclusion of a cross reference instruction at both three-character category headings of the principal and extended category. For example:

Principal category
E02   Plastic operations on nose
  Note: Principal category, extended at E07

Extended category
E07   Other plastic operations on nose
  Note: Principal E02

Extended categories are not always in numerical order but have sometimes been slotted into gaps within the classification.

PRule 6: Retired categories and codes

Retired categories and codes must not be used.

Codes fall out of favour for various reasons and there is a mechanism, called retiring, for handling such codes. However, the retirement of a code is only ever considered as a very last option. If an extraordinary circumstance arises where a code/description is considered invalid (usually following classification review), the code, the associated problem, an options appraisal to address it and recommendation(s) are provided to the OPCS-4 Editorial Board for a decision. The support of the relevant professional body would also be required in these circumstances to provide appropriate clinical input.

In practice, the code is retired in the classification with a note to that effect and excluded from the metadata file (used by hospital coding systems) so that it is no longer perpetuated. Additionally, the successor code and the retired code are mapped in the Table of Coding Equivalence (used to analyse the equivalent codes in the current and previous releases of OPCS-4).

The following categories/codes have been retired from OPCS-4:

M06.4	**Code retired**	**- refer to introduction**
R03	**Category retired**	**- refer to introduction**
X15.3	**Code retired**	**- refer to introduction**
X63	**Category retired**	**- refer to introduction**
X64	**Category retired**	**- refer to introduction**

PRule 7: Subsidiary Chapters Y and Z

Codes from the subsidiary Chapters **Y Subsidiary Classification of Methods of Operation** and **Z Subsidiary Classification of Sites of Operation** must only ever be coded in a secondary position.

Codes from the subsidiary Chapters **Y Subsidiary Classification of Methods of Operation** and **Z Subsidiary Classification of Sites of Operation** are used to supplement codes from other chapters.

Codes from Chapter Y are used to enhance codes from the body system chapters where this adds further information about the intervention/procedure that cannot be fully reflected by the assignment of the body system code alone.

PRule 7: *continued*

Codes from Chapter Z are used to define more specifically the site of the operation. Chapter Z also contains codes to identify the laterality of a procedure, e.g. right sided operation, left sided operation and bilateral operation.

Detailed standards on the use of these subsidiary chapters are provided in Chapter Y and Chapter Z.

PRule 8: Surgical eponyms

Section II Alphabetical Index of Surgical Eponyms within Volume II – Alphabetical Index must only be used as a guide when coding.

Where an eponym is used in the medical record the coder must analyse the procedural information and ensure that code assignment fully reflects the procedure performed.

Where the coder is unsure what procedure the eponym describes, they must seek advice from the responsible consultant to ensure that the correct codes are assigned.

A surgical eponym is a procedure either named after the surgeon who pioneered it, or the device used within it. Another surgeon may later adapt the procedure in some way; thereby varying from the original procedure describing the original eponym. The use of eponyms is discouraged for the purpose of OPCS-4 code assignment, and such terms are excluded from Section I of the Alphabetical Index and the Tabular List.

Section II Alphabetical Index of Surgical Eponyms within the Alphabetical Index is a list of eponyms and suggested codes to be used to classify the procedure. This section is provided in recognition of the fact that clinicians still write these in the medical record.

This section was not significantly revised in either OPCS-4.4 or subsequent releases, therefore not all eponyms in current usage will be listed.

Some eponyms are listed more than once and the code given may be different in each case because the eponym describes two different procedures or the surgeon may have developed a number of different devices.

The abbreviation (D) at the end of an eponym description denotes device and the code assigned is that allocated for the insertion of the device.

A bracketed Z code (Z) following the procedure description indicates the necessary site code to be added.

PRule 9: Surgical abbreviations

Section III Alphabetical Index of Surgical Abbreviations within Volume II – Alphabetical Index must only be used as a guide when coding.

Where an abbreviation is used in the medical record the coder must analyse the procedural information and ensure that code and it's description fully reflects the procedure performed.

Where the coder is unsure what procedure the abbreviation describes they must seek advice from the responsible consultant to ensure that the correct codes are assigned.

Section III Alphabetical Index of Surgical Abbreviations within the Alphabetical Index contains a short alphabetical index of abbreviations of procedures and interventions. As well as listing the abbreviation itself, this section contains the relevant OPCS-4 code and its description. This list is not exhaustive and does not contain all abbreviations in current usage.

PRule 10: National Tariff High Cost Drugs List

The National Tariff High Cost Drugs List (HCD) contains the High Cost Drugs which are excluded from the National Tariff Payment System. The HCD List is reviewed and updated on an annual basis.

The Terminology and Classifications Delivery Service issues the High Cost Drugs Clinical Coding Standards as the national organisation responsible for clinical coding guidance and setting national classifications standards in use in the NHS.

The maps to OPCS-4 categories and their subcategories are provided to produce the DH High Cost Drugs List so that clinical coders can assign an appropriate OPCS-4 code.

See PCSX22: High Cost Drugs (X81–X98) and, for full standards for coding high cost drugs refer to the National Tariff High Cost Drugs List and High Cost Drugs Clinical Coding Standards and Guidance which can be downloaded from the Main Publications page on Delen.

PRule 11: National Tariff Chemotherapy Regimens List

The National Tariff Chemotherapy Regimens List is published to enable the collection, reporting and costing of chemotherapy regimens in the NHS in England.

The Terminology and Classifications Delivery Service issue the Chemotherapy Regimen Clinical Coding Standards as a separate document as the national organisation responsible for clinical coding guidance and setting the national classifications standards in use in the NHS.

The Chemotherapy Regimens List is an alphabetical list by common regimen abbreviation. The list includes all of the regimens that are in common use in the UK. Each regimen is mapped to an OPCS-4 code for procurement and a code for delivery (administration) of the chemotherapy so that clinical coders can assign the appropriate OPCS-4 code.

See PCSX21: Procurement and delivery of drugs for chemotherapy for neoplasm (X70–X74) and, for full standards for coding chemotherapy refer to the National Tariff Chemotherapy Regimens List and Chemotherapy Regimens Clinical Coding Standards and Guidance which can be downloaded from the Main Publications page on Delen.

CONVENTIONS OF OPCS-4

PConvention 1: Cross references

Cross references are provided in the Alphabetical Index to ensure that all possible terms are referenced by the coder. Cross references explicitly direct the coder to other entries in the index:

See

This is an explicit direction to look elsewhere.

See also

This is a reminder to look under another lead term if all the information cannot be found under the first lead term entry.

PConvention 2: Instructional notes and paired codes

Instructional 'Notes' are used within the Tabular list at chapter level, three-character and four-character levels. There are three types of notes:

Includes notes

Includes notes clarify the content (intent) of the chapter, category or subcategory to which the note applies. It states exactly what is included within the chapter, category or subcategory.

Excludes notes

Excludes notes are used to prevent a category from being used incorrectly. They direct the coder away from an incorrect code and direct to the correct code. A specific reference to the correct chapter, category or subcategory is listed in brackets following the exclusion statement.

Note

Notes provide instructions for coding and may be used:

- to advise coders to include or omit additional or subsidiary codes

- to direct coders elsewhere in the classification for more appropriate categories

- to clarify the intended use of codes in a particular chapter, category or subcategory

- to provide specific instruction on the correct sequencing of codes when used together (**paired codes**).

Paired codes notes

Some interventions/procedures are frequently carried out together but are classified at separate codes or categories. Where this is the case the categories concerned contain instructional **Notes** to indicate the associated code and correct sequencing.

The following paired codes notes appear in the OPCS-4 Tabular List:

- 'Use **a** supplementary code/Use **an** additional code/Use **a** subsidiary code' – **use the code this note appears at in _primary_ position**.

- 'Use **as** a supplementary code/Use **as an** additional code/For use as a subsidiary code, Use **as a** secondary code' – **use the code this note appears at in a _secondary_ position**.

Paired codes may be classified within the same or a different body system chapter. They can be used alone when only one intervention/procedure is performed.

PConvention 3: Abbreviations

The following abbreviations are used in the Tabular List and the Alphabetical Index:

HFQ (However Further Qualified)

Signifies that a statement may be further qualified/described in a number of ways, which will not affect the code assignment, It refers to the part of the procedural statement that immediately precedes the abbreviation HFQ; it therefore makes no difference how much more specific the clinician is in their statement, there is only one code option for that intervention in OPCS-4.

NEC (Not Elsewhere Classified)

Indicates that a more detailed variation of the term may be covered by another code. Sometimes the more detailed code is found within the same three-character category. If a more detailed code is not available then the NEC code is assigned.

NFQ (Not Further Qualified)

Signifies the statement written by the clinician has no further description provided. In effect it is an 'unspecified' statement.

NOC (Not Otherwise Classifiable)

Is used only in the subsidiary Chapter Y and indicates these methods of operation codes are to be used only when they cannot be specifically coded (i.e. not classified) to any chapter in the main classification.

Two other abbreviations found in the tabular list are the symbols:

>	Greater than
<	Less than

Examples:

Patient admitted for left sided hemicolectomy and formation of loop ileostomy

> **H09.4   Left hemicolectomy and ileostomy HFQ**
> The HFQ applies to the ileostomy. It doesn't matter how the ileostomy is further qualified, i.e. whether it's a loop ileostomy or an end ileostomy, the code is still the same

Patient admitted for endoscopic sphincterotomy of sphincter of Oddi and balloon trawl and removal of calculus

> **J38.1   Endoscopic sphincterotomy of sphincter of Oddi and removal of calculus HFQ**
> The HFQ applies to the removal of calculus. It doesn't matter how the removal of the calculus is further qualified; i.e. the calculus could be extracted using a balloon or a basket, the code is still the same

Patient admitted for secondary open reduction and fixation of the right lateral malleolus fracture using extramedullary plate

> **W23.2   Secondary open reduction of fracture of bone and extramedullary fixation HFQ**
> The HFQ applies to the extramedullary fixation. It doesn't matter how the fixation device is further qualified, e.g. nail or screw, or in this instance a plate, the code is still the same

GENERAL CODING STANDARDS AND GUIDANCE

PGCS1: Endoscopic and minimal access operations that do not have a specific code

When an endoscopic or minimally invasive procedure (i.e. arthroscopic, thoracoscopic and laparoscopic) is undertaken but no specific code exists to capture this type of approach, dual coding is required. The following codes and sequencing is required:

- Open procedure code

- **Y74–Y76** minimal access approach code

  - When more than one minimally invasive procedure has been undertaken an approach code must be assigned after each open procedure code

- Chapter Y Subsidiary Classification of Methods of Operation code (if required)

- Chapter Z site code(s)

- **Z94.- Laterality of operation** (if applicable)

The Tabular List of the classification includes a range of categories designated as 'endoscopic' procedures, e.g. **M42 Endoscopic extirpation of lesion of bladder**.

When the classification was constructed it was intended that these categories would be primarily used for operations carried out through existing anatomical passages. However, in the past, some of these categories were also expected to be used for operations carried out using minimal incisions through which rigid or fibreoptic scopes are introduced into body cavities, e.g. **Q37 Endoscopic reversal of female sterilisation**.

This practice was maintained in subsequent versions of OPCS-4 and further specific categories were introduced to differentiate between endoscopic and laparoscopic, e.g. **J17.1 Endoscopic ultrasound examination of liver and biopsy of lesion of liver and J09.3 Laparoscopic ultrasound examination of liver NEC**.

Examples:

Endoscopic dacryocystorhinostomy

C25.4	**Dacryocystorhinostomy NEC**
Y76.3	**Endoscopic approach to other body cavity**

Endoscopic primary repair of flexor digitorum profundus (FDP) tendon of left arm using graft

T67.5	**Primary repair of tendon using graft**
Y76.3	**Endoscopic approach to other body cavity**
Z56.4	**Flexor digitorum profundus**
Z94.3	**Left sided operation**

Arthroscopic (endoscopic) capsulorrhaphy left shoulder

W81.6	**Capsulorrhaphy of joint**
Y76.7	**Arthroscopic approach to joint**
Z81.4	**Shoulder joint**
Z94.3	**Left sided operation**

Laparoscopic repair of left inguinal hernia using insert of natural material and a laparoscopic repair of umbilical hernia using sutures performed at the same time during the same theatre visit

T20.1	**Primary repair of inguinal hernia using insert of natural material**
Y75.2	**Laparoscopic approach to abdominal cavity NEC**
Z94.3	**Left sided operation**
T24.3	**Repair of umbilical hernia using sutures**
Y75.2	**Laparoscopic approach to abdominal cavity NEC**

Laparoscopic total abdominal hysterectomy with laparoscopic bilateral salpingoophorectomy performed at the same time during the same theatre visit

Q07.4	**Total abdominal hysterectomy NEC**
	Note: Use a supplementary code for concurrent excision of ovary and/or fallopian tube (Q22–Q24)
Y75.2	**Laparoscopic approach to abdominal cavity NEC**
Q22.1	**Bilateral salpingoophorectomy**
Y75.2	**Laparoscopic approach to abdominal cavity NEC**

Laparoscopic excision of endometriosis of pouch of Douglas

P31.8	**Other specified operations on pouch of Douglas**
Y75.2	**Laparoscopic approach to abdominal cavity NEC**
Y06.9	**Unspecified excision of lesion of organ NOC**

Laparoscopic deroofing of cyst of the right kidney and laparoscopic denervation of the right kidney

M04.1	**Deroofing of cyst of kidney**
Y75.2	**Laparoscopic approach to abdominal cavity NEC**
M08.2	**Open denervation of kidney**
Y75.2	**Laparoscopic approach to abdominal cavity NEC**
Z94.2	**Right sided operation**

PGCS2: Diagnostic versus therapeutic procedures

If a diagnostic procedure proceeds to, or is performed *at the same time* as, a therapeutic procedure *on the same site* then only the code for the therapeutic procedure is required. This includes:

- diagnostic endoscopies performed prior to an open procedure

- diagnostic endoscopies performed prior to a **therapeutic endoscopic** procedure (as indicated by the instructional **Notes** at all therapeutic endoscopic codes).

When a diagnostic (exploratory) laparotomy performed to search for possible pathology progresses to therapeutic procedure(s) as a result of the exploration, only the therapeutic procedure(s) is coded.

There are exceptions to this standard, for example (this is not a definitive list):

- ERCP (**J43**) together with sphincterotomy of sphincter of Oddi (**J38**) (as indicated by the **Note** at the headings of these categories)

- D&C together with diagnostic hysteroscopy and intrauterine coil (***See PCSQ2: Dilation, curettage (D&C), hysteroscopy and intrauterine coil (Q10.3, Q10.8, Q18.8, Q18.9, Q12)***)

- Therapeutic endoscopic procedures (excluding excisions) with biopsy (***see PGCS10: Coding endoscopic procedures***).

PGCS2: *continued*

If there is any doubt as to whether a procedure is diagnostic or therapeutic, clarification must be sought from the responsible consultant.

See also PGCS9: Excision and biopsy procedures.

Examples:

Colonoscopy to the descending colon due to rectal bleed reveals a tumour in the descending colon, the surgeon immediately proceeds to left hemicolectomy and end to end anastomosis of colon to rectum.

H09.1   Left hemicolectomy and end to end anastomosis of colon to rectum

Only code the therapeutic procedure because the surgeon proceeded to a therapeutic procedure after a diagnostic procedure on the same site, during the same visit to theatre.

Excision of lesion of skin of the right temple and shave biopsy of lesion of skin of nose during the same visit to theatre.

S06.5   Excision of lesion of skin of head or neck NEC
Z47.2   Skin of temple
Z94.2   Right sided operation
E09.5   Biopsy of lesion of external nose
S14.1   Shave biopsy of lesion of skin of head or neck

Code both the therapeutic and diagnostic procedure as these were performed on two different sites.

Acute abdominal pain. An exploratory laparotomy reveals ruptured right ovarian cyst. Marsupialisation of ovarian lesion performed.

Q43.3   Marsupialisation of lesion of ovary
Z94.2   Right sided operation

Only assign the codes for the marsupialisation of the right ovarian cyst, because the exploratory laparotomy progressed to a therapeutic procedure.

PGCS3: Incomplete, unfinished, abandoned and failed procedures

Abandoned, failed or incomplete procedures (excludes failed procedures converted to open, ***see PGCS4: Failed percutaneous and minimal access procedures converted to open***) must be coded to the stage reached at the abandonment of the procedure; the intention must not be coded. However, if the intervention/procedure reaches the final stage and has been unsuccessful, it must be coded as if the whole procedure has been carried out.

The exception to this standard is ***PCSJ2: Failed or abandoned endoscopic retrograde cholangiopancreatography (J43.9).***

Examples:

Patient admitted for fibreoptic gastroscopy. Procedure abandoned due to obstruction in the oesophagus. Scope could not progress beyond the obstruction

G16.9   Unspecified diagnostic fibreoptic endoscopic examination of oesophagus

Patient with carcinoma stomach admitted for partial gastrectomy. Procedure commenced but carcinoma found to be inoperable

T30.9   Unspecified opening of abdomen
        Includes: Exploratory laparotomy NEC

Patient admitted for endoscopic retrograde cholangiopancreatography (ERCP) and endoscopic incision of sphincter of Oddi for removal of bile duct calculus by dormia basket. Extraction attempted, but consultant unable to remove calculus during the procedure

> **J38.1   Endoscopic sphincterotomy of sphincter of Oddi and removal of calculus HFQ**
> *Note:* ***Use a supplementary code for concurrent diagnostic endoscopic retrograde examination of bile duct and pancreatic duct (J43)***
>
> **J43.9   Unspecified diagnostic endoscopic retrograde examination of bile duct and pancreatic duct**
> *Includes: Endoscopic retrograde cholangiopancreatography NEC*
> *Note:* ***Use as a supplementary code when associated with endoscopic incision of sphincter of Oddi (J38)***

This procedure must be coded as though it has been carried out as it has reached the final stage at time of abandonment.

PGCS4: Failed percutaneous and minimal access procedures converted to open

When a minimal access or percutaneous transluminal approach procedure fails and is converted to an open procedure, during the same visit to theatre, the following codes and sequencing must be applied:

- Open procedure code

- **Y71.4 Failed minimal access approach converted to open** or **Y71.5 Failed percutaneous transluminal approach converted to open**

Examples:

Failed laparoscopic cholecystectomy, converted to an open cholecystectomy

> **J18.3   Total cholecystectomy NEC**
> *Includes: Cholecystectomy NEC*
> **Y71.4   Failed minimal access approach converted to open**

Percutaneous transluminal embolisation of renal artery failed converted to an open embolisation of renal artery

> **L42.2   Open embolisation of renal artery**
> **Y71.5   Failed percutaneous transluminal approach converted to open**

PGCS5: Unintentional procedures

Where an unintentional action, such as perforation of an organ, occurs during a procedure, this unintentional action must **not** be recorded using OPCS-4 codes. The unintentional action must be coded using the appropriate ICD-10 code from the range **T80–T88 Complications of surgical and medical care, not elsewhere classified**.

Any surgical procedures performed after the unintentional injury, e.g. suture of accidentally perforated organ, must be recorded using the appropriate OPCS-4 code(s). It is possible that the procedure carried out on the injured organ may become the primary procedure if it becomes the main procedure carried out.

Examples:

Patient admitted for excision of their gall bladder, whilst accessing the abdominal cavity the pancreas was accidentally lacerated which was sutured. Successful removal of the gall bladder followed.

> **J18.3   Total cholecystectomy NEC**
> **J65.8   Other specified other open operations on pancreas**
> **Y25.1   Suture of laceration of organ NOC**

Patient taken to theatre for endoscopic endometrial ablation; during an initial hysteroscopy a perforation of the uterus occurs. Laparotomy was performed and a subtotal abdominal excision of the uterus was carried out. Endometrial ablation was not performed.

    Q07.5   Subtotal abdominal hysterectomy

PGCS6: Radical operations

When coding radical operations:

- Code assignment must fully reflect the procedure(s) performed during the radical operation

- Instructional **Notes** must be applied in order to fully reflect all procedures performed

- Any uncertainty as to what procedures were performed during the radical operation must be clarified with the responsible consultant in order to ensure correct code assignment.

Radical operations generally involve procedures on multiple sites. These may include the removal of blood supply, lymph nodes and adjacent structures of a diseased organ and are often used in the treatment of malignant neoplasms.

Radical operations are generally not listed in the Alphabetical index or the Tabular list of OPCS-4.

Examples:

Radical mastectomy involving total removal of left breast, both pectoral muscles and block dissection of axillary lymph nodes

    B27.2   Total mastectomy and excision of both pectoral muscles NEC
                    Note: Use a supplementary code for removal of lymph node (T85–T87)
    T85.2   Block dissection of axillary lymph nodes
    Z94.3   Left sided operation

Radical right nephrectomy with excision of perirenal tissue and adrenal gland

    M02.1   Nephrectomy and excision of perirenal tissue
    Z94.2   Right sided operation
    B22.3   Unilateral adrenalectomy
    Z94.2   Right sided operation

PGCS7: Resection and reconstruction procedures

Where resection and reconstruction have been performed the codes that classify the resection must be assigned before the codes that classify the reconstruction.

PGCS8: Incision as a means of approach

When incisions are made as a means of approach in order to perform further surgery on the site, the incision itself must not be coded.

Examples:

Laparotomy with excision of cyst of left ovary

    Q43.2   Excision of lesion of ovary
    Z94.3   Left sided operation

Incision and drainage of lesion of skin of right leg

    S47.2   Drainage of lesion of skin NEC
    Z50.4   Skin of leg NEC
    Z94.2   Right sided operation

PGCS9: Excision and biopsy procedures

When an excision and biopsy is performed on the *same* site during the *same* theatre visit (often referred to as an excision biopsy), only assign a code(s) for the excision, as a biopsy is an integral part of the excision.

PGCS10: Coding endoscopic procedures

Diagnostic endoscopic procedures

Where multiple organs are examined during a diagnostic endoscopy, a site code from Chapter Z must be added to identify the furthest site examined (the sites included at each category are indicated at the category *includes* notes).

During a diagnostic endoscopy if a biopsy is performed at the same time as other multiple sites are examined, the site of the biopsy is of greater importance than the other sites examined and the site of the biopsy is the only site code required. This includes if the site of biopsy is not the furthest site examined.

Where multiple biopsies are taken, it is only necessary to site code the furthest point biopsied.

Therapeutic endoscopic procedures

The standard in *PGCS2: Diagnostic versus therapeutic procedures* applies to therapeutic endoscopic procedures with the exception of therapeutic endoscopic procedures (that is not an excision) with biopsy.

When a therapeutic endoscopic procedure is performed that is **not an excision** and a biopsy is taken at the same time, from **the same or a different site**, the following codes and sequencing must be applied:

- Therapeutic endoscopy code
- Chapter Z site code (if the therapeutic endoscopy code does not state the site of the procedure or where the site of the biopsy is different to the therapeutic endoscopy)
- **Y20 Biopsy of organ NOC**
- Chapter Z site code (for the site of the biopsy)

When an **endoscopic excision** is performed and a biopsy is taken at the same time, the biopsy must only be coded if it is taken from a **different site** to the excision (the sites included at each category are indicated at the category *includes* notes), using the following codes and sequencing:

- Endoscopic excision code
- Chapter Z site code (if doing so adds further information)
- **Y20 Biopsy of organ NOC**
- Chapter Z site code (for the site of the biopsy)

See PGCS9: Excision and biopsy procedures.

When other sites have been passed in order to arrive at the point of the actual therapeutic endoscopic procedure the assumption is that all the sites en route to the point of the procedure are examined and therefore must not be identified separately.

Where multiple excisions have been performed site codes must be assigned for each site of excision (the sites included at each category are indicated at the category *includes* notes).

PGCS10: *continued*

There are two types of endoscopic procedures:

Diagnostic – the endoscope is used to examine the organ in order to determine the nature of the disease

Therapeutic – the endoscope is used to administer some form of treatment for the disease.

The 'endoscopy NEC' default in OPCS-4 is fibreoptic (flexible) as this accurately reflects clinical practice, i.e. where the type of endoscope has not been stated, the classification defaults the coder to a fibreoptic category.

Examples:

Endoscopic examination of gastrointestinal tract to pylorus

G45.9 **Unspecified diagnostic fibreoptic endoscopic examination of upper gastrointestinal tract**
Includes: Diagnostic endoscopic examination of upper gastrointestinal tract NEC
Oesophagus
Stomach
Pylorus
Proximal duodenum
Note: Use a subsidiary site code as necessary

Z27.3 **Pylorus**

Endoscopic examination of trachea, bronchus and lung with biopsy of trachea

E49.1 **Diagnostic fibreoptic endoscopic examination of lower respiratory tract and biopsy of lesion of lower respiratory tract**
Includes: Diagnostic endoscopic examination of lower respiratory tract NEC
Trachea
Carina
Bronchus
Lung
Note: Use a subsidiary site code as necessary

Z24.3 **Trachea**

Fibreoptic endoscopic examination of upper gastrointestinal tract with biopsies of oesophagus and stomach

G45.1 **Fibreoptic endoscopic examination of upper gastrointestinal tract and biopsy of lesion of upper gastrointestinal tract**
Includes: Diagnostic endoscopic examination of upper gastrointestinal tract NEC
Oesophagus
Stomach
Pylorus
Proximal duodenum
Note: Use a subsidiary site code as necessary

Z27.2 **Stomach**

Fibreoptic endoscopy to stomach with removal of foreign body from oesophagus and biopsy of oesophagus

> **G44.2** **Fibreoptic removal of foreign body from upper gastrointestinal tract**
> *Includes:* *Diagnostic endoscopic examination of upper gastrointestinal tract NEC*
> *Oesophagus*
> *Stomach*
> *Pylorus*
> *Proximal duodenum*
> **Note: Use a subsidiary site code as necessary**

> **Y20.9** **Unspecified biopsy of organ NOC**
> **Z27.1** **Oesophagus**

Fibreoptic endoscopic removal of foreign body from trachea and biopsy of lung

> **E48.5** **Fibreoptic endoscopic removal of foreign body from lower respiratory tract**
> *Includes:* *Therapeutic endoscopic operations on lower respiratory tract NEC*
> *Trachea*
> *Carina*
> *Bronchus*
> *Lung*
> **Note: It is not necessary to code additionally any mention of diagnostic fibreoptic endoscopic examination of lower respiratory tract (E49.9)**
> **Note: Use a subsidiary site code as necessary**

> **Z24.3** **Trachea**
> **Y20.9** **Unspecified biopsy of organ NOC**
> **Z24.6** **Lung**

Colonoscopy with snare excision of lesions of caecum, and biopsy of transverse colon

> **H20.1** **Fibreoptic endoscopic snare resection of lesion of colon**
> *Includes:* *Caecum*
> *Mucosa of colon*
> *Mucosa of caecum*
> **Note: Use a subsidiary site code as necessary**

> **Z28.2** **Caecum**
> **Y20.9** **Unspecified biopsy of organ NOC**
> **Z28.4** **Transverse colon**

Endoscopic snare resection of lesion of sigmoid colon and biopsy of lesion of sigmoid colon:

> **H23.1** **Endoscopic snare resection of lesion of lower bowel using fibreoptic sigmoidoscope**
> *Includes:* *Endoscopic extirpation of lesion of lower bowel NEC*
> *Sigmoid colon*
> *Colon*
> *Rectum*
> **Note: Use a subsidiary site code as necessary**

> **Z28.6** **Sigmoid colon**

Fibreoptic endoscopic cauterisation of lesion of the pylorus. The oesophagus and stomach are examined en route.

G43.3   Fibreoptic endoscopic cauterisation of lesion of upper gastrointestinal tract
Includes: Endoscopic extirpation of lesion of upper gastrointestinal tract NEC
Oesophagus
Stomach
Pylorus
Proximal duodenum
Note: Use a subsidiary site code as necessary
Z27.3   Pylorus

Colonoscopy with snare excision of lesions from caecum, transverse and sigmoid colon

H20.1   Fibreoptic endoscopic snare resection of lesion of colon
Includes: Caecum
Mucosa of colon
Mucosa of caecum
Note: Use a subsidiary site code as necessary
Z28.2   Caecum
Z28.4   Transverse colon
Z28.6   Sigmoid colon

PGCS11: Coding procedures performed for the correction of congenital deformities

When coding procedures performed for the correction of congenital deformities the following apply:

- If the Chapter X code can be directly index trailed from the OPCS-4 Alphabetical Index (Volume II), then the Chapter X code **must** be used.

- If a code that more accurately reflects the procedure can be found elsewhere within the main body system Chapters (A–W), the code(s) from the main body system chapter(s) must be used, unless there is a specific instruction to do otherwise.

- The coder must ensure that the codes assigned fully and accurately describe the procedure(s) performed and it may, therefore, be appropriate to seek advice from the responsible clinician.

Certain procedures performed to correct congenital deformities are classified within Chapter X and Chapter W of OPCS-4. The Chapter X codes for the correction of congenital deformities are very specific and encompass the diagnosis for which the procedure is being carried out within the category title.

The '**Excludes**' notes which exist at some categories in Chapter W state that *'some similar operations for correction of congenital deformity'* are classified in Chapter X. These notes **do not** indicate that a code from Chapter X must always be used when coding a procedure for the correction of a congenital condition.

When coding procedures performed for the correction of congenital deformities the ICD-10 diagnosis code is used as a parameter to confirm the fact that the deformity is congenital.

Examples:

Separation of tarsal coalition of left foot.

X25.4   Separation of tarsal coalition
Z94.3   Left sided operation

The OPCS-4 Alphabetical Index (Volume II) specifically directs to code **X25.4 Separation of tarsal coalition**.

Second stage tendo-achilles tenotomy and resiting of wire proximal ring of Ilizarov fixator (inserted at 1st stage) of right foot for correction of congenital clubfoot

T70.2	**Tenotomy NEC**
Y71.1	**Subsequent stage of staged operations NOC**
Z58.1	**Triceps surae**
W30.2	**Adjustment to external fixation of bone NEC**
Z80.9	**Bone of foot NEC**
Z94.2	**Right sided operation**

The OPCS-4 Alphabetical Index (Volume II) directs the coder directly to OPCS-4 codes outside of Chapter X. These codes more accurately reflect the procedure than codes within Chapter X.

PGCS12: Coding grafts and harvests of sites other than skin

Grafts (other than skin grafts) must be coded as follows:

Autografts (graft using material harvested from patient):

- Body system chapter code classifying the organ/site being grafted*

- Chapter Z site code identifying the specific site/organ being grafted (if this has not already been identified within the body system code)

- **Z94.- Laterality of operation** (if applicable)

- Chapter Y code identifying the type of tissue harvested and the site of harvest (unless this is identified within the body system code)

- Chapter Z site code identifying the site of the harvest (if this has not already been identified within the Y harvest code)

- **Z94.- Laterality of operation** (if applicable).

*Even if the body system code description does not contain the term 'graft' it is not necessary to assign a code from **Y27.- Graft to organ NOC**, as the graft is implied with the assignment of the harvest code.

Other types of graft (grafts using material not harvested from patient, including allograft, xenograft and prosthetic graft):

- Body system chapter code classifying the organ/site being grafted

- **Y27.- Graft to organ NOC** if a graft and/or the material used has not been identified within the body system code

- Chapter Z site code identifying the specific site/organ being grafted (if this has not already been identified within the body system code)

- **Z94.- Laterality of operation** (if applicable).

An additional harvest code must not be assigned.

The exception to this standard is *PCSW4: Total hip replacement with acetabular bone graft (W37-W39)*.

See also:

- *PCSS3: Coding skin grafts and harvests*

- *PCSW3: Harvest of bone marrow for autologous transplant (W35.8)*

- *PCSX12: Donation of skin (X46.2)*

- *PCSY12: Donor status (Y99)*

Examples:

Primary graft to right femoral nerve. Patient's right sural nerve harvested.

A63.1	**Primary graft to peripheral nerve NEC**
Z10.1	**Femoral nerve**
Z94.2	**Right sided operation**
Y54.1	**Harvest of sural nerve**
Z94.2	**Right sided operation**

Autograft bone from left iliac crest to right radius

W31.9	**Unspecified other autograft of bone**
Z70.9	**Radius NEC**
Z94.2	**Right sided operation**
Y66.3	**Harvest of bone from iliac crest**
Z94.3	**Left sided operation**

Left tympanoplasty using left tragus graft

D14.1	**Tympanoplasty using graft**
Z94.3	**Left sided operation**
Y69.2	**Harvest of cartilage from ear**
Z94.3	**Left sided operation**

Endoscopic replacement of right meniscus using allograft from cadaver

W82.8	**Other specified therapeutic endoscopic operations on semilunar cartilage**
Y01.6	**Alloreplacement of organ from cadaver NOC**
Z94.2	**Right sided operation**

Bypass of one coronary artery using saphenous vein graft

K40.1	**Saphenous vein graft replacement of one coronary artery**

PGCS14: Sequencing of codes in Chapter Y with codes in Chapter Z

When assigning codes from both **Chapter Y Subsidiary Classification of Methods of Operation** and **Chapter Z Subsidiary Classification of Sites of Operation** the Chapter Y code must precede the Chapter Z code.

PGCS15: Emergency procedures

When deciding which category to assign, the nature of the *procedure* and not the nature of the *admission* must be taken into account. The term *emergency* pertains to the use of operating theatre time that has not been pre-scheduled (including operations added to a pre-scheduled list). If there is any doubt, the coder must seek advice from the responsible consultant

Separate categories exist within **Chapter H Lower Digestive Tract, Chapter L Arteries and Veins** and **Chapter R Female Genital Tract Associated with Pregnancy, Childbirth and Puerperium** to classify emergency and other excision of appendix (Chapter H) or emergency and other replacement/bypass of artery (Chapter L) or elective and other caesarean delivery (Chapter R).

Example:

Patient admitted from outpatient clinic with large infrarenal abdominal aortic aneurysm. Added to that afternoon's surgical theatre list for a replacement of aneurysmal segment by anastomosis of aorta to aorta.

> **L18.4   Emergency replacement of aneurysmal segment of infrarenal abdominal aorta by anastomosis of aorta to aorta**

> The terms **revision** and **revisional** are used to allow discrimination between subsequent operations on the *same* site usually to correct or remove a problem arising since the original surgery, and operations of a primary nature with the same name. Procedures which involve the use of a prosthesis are only considered a revision where this is a 'like for like' procedure.

Examples:

Replacement of an uncemented left Freeman total hip replacement with an uncemented Monk prosthesis

> **W38.3   Revision of total prosthetic replacement of hip joint not using cement**
> **Z94.3   Left sided operation**

> This is a like for like procedure because the uncemented prosthesis is replaced with another uncemented prosthesis, it is therefore coded as a revision.

Revisional septoplasty of the nose

> **E03.6   Septoplasty of nose NEC**
> **Y71.3   Revisional operations NOC**

PGCS16: Conversion procedures

'Conversion to' and 'Conversion from' codes must always be:

- sequenced with the 'Conversion to' code preceding the 'Conversion from' code

- used together, except where there is a note indicating that a code not specifically described as a 'conversion to' or conversion from' can be used

- assigned from *different* three-character categories.

'Conversion' procedures relate to the dismantling of a particular type of operation and the introduction of a 'new' and 'different' procedure on the same site.

The new procedure is coded as a 'conversion to' procedure. The 'conversion from' code, always ends in **.0**, and represents the previous procedure being dismantled.

Conversion codes can be found at Chapters G and W.

Examples:

Conversion to left total hip replacement (THR) using cement from a previous uncemented THR.

> **W37.2   Conversion to total prosthetic replacement of hip joint using cement**
> > ***Note: Use a subsidiary conversion from code as necessary***
> **W38.0   Conversion from previous uncemented total prosthetic replacement of hip joint**
> **Z94.3   Left sided operation**

Conversion from a direct anastomosis of oesophagus to a bypass of oesophagus by interposition of jejunum.

G05.4	**Bypass of oesophagus by interposition of jejunum NEC**
G06.0	**Conversion from previous direct anastomosis of oesophagus**

> *Note:* ***For use as a subsidiary code when associated with construction of interposition anastomosis of oesophagus (G05)***

> The term **secondary** is used to identify a repeated procedure on the *same* site. It may identify a secondary treatment/procedure which is different from the original, but which is performed for the same purpose as the original procedure.
>
> *See also PCSW1: **Secondary reduction and remanipulation of fracture and fracture dislocation.***

Example:

Secondary repair of right extensor hallucis longus tendon using lengthening procedure

T68.2	**Secondary repair of tendon using lengthening procedure**
Z58.5	**Extensor hallucis longus**
Z94.2	**Right sided operation**

PGCS17: Maintenance and attention to procedures

A supplementary code from Chapter Y must be added in addition to the maintenance/attention to code, when doing so provides additional information.

Maintenance and attention to codes are used when a further procedure is carried out on an existing procedure that cannot be classified to a dedicated code within that category. A supplementary code from Chapter Y must be added in addition to the attention to/maintenance code, when doing so provides additional information.

Examples:

Resiting of urethral catheter in bladder

M47.5	**Maintenance of urethral catheter in bladder**
Y03.4	**Other resiting of prosthesis in organ NOC**

Correction of displaced right cochlear prosthesis:

D24.3	**Attention to cochlear prosthesis**
Y03.3	**Correction of displacement of prosthesis NOC**
Z94.2	**Right sided operation**

PGCS18: Staged procedures

When coding staged procedures, if a specific code describing the staged procedure is not available one of the following codes must be assigned as an additional code to indicate the stage of the procedure:

Y70.3	**First stage of staged operations NOC**
Y71.1	**Subsequent stage of staged operations NOC**

Some procedures are performed in planned separate stages where the patient undergoes the first stage of the procedure during one visit to theatre and then undergoes the second and subsequent procedure(s) at a later date. Specific codes are available in some of the body system chapters that classify procedures that are commonly performed in separate stages e.g. **D05.1 First stage insertion of fixtures for auricular prosthesis, E11.3 Second stage attachment of fixtures for nasal prosthesis, N08.3 First stage bilateral orchidopexy** etc. Not all procedures that can be performed in stages have dedicated staged procedure codes.

Examples:

Patient admitted for first stage of a two stage repair of cleft palate

> **F29.1** **Primary repair of cleft palate**
> **Y70.3** **First stage of staged operations NOC**

Patient admitted for second stage of repair of cleft palate

> **F29.1** **Primary repair of cleft palate**
> **Y71.1** **Subsequent stage of staged operations NOC**

PGCS19: Temporary operations

Where a temporary operation is performed and a specific temporary operation code does not exist, code **Y70.5 Temporary operations** must be assigned in a secondary position.

Code **Y44.3 Temporary occlusion of organ NOC** must be used in preference to **Y70.5** if an organ is temporarily occluded.

Various codes exist within OPCS-4 which specifically classify a temporary operation, for example:

> **G74.2** **Creation of temporary ileostomy**
> **X42.1** **Insertion of temporary peritoneal dialysis catheter**

Example:

Temporary implantation of intravenous single chamber pacemaker under fluoroscopic control

> **K60.5** **Implantation of intravenous single chamber cardiac pacemaker system**
> **Y53.4** **Approach to organ under fluoroscopic control**
> **Y70.5** **Temporary operations**

Enhancing body system codes using codes from Chapter S

Codes from Chapter S may be used to enhance codes from other body system chapter. ***See PChSS1: Enhancing body system codes using codes from Chapter S.***

Coding diagnostic imaging procedures classified outside of Chapter U

When a specific code classifying a diagnostic imaging procedure is available in a body system chapter (Chapters A-T and V–W) the body system chapter code **must** be used in preference to the codes within categories **U01–U21** and **U35–U37**.

See PCSU1: Diagnostic imaging procedures (U01–U21 and U35–U37)

Coding radiotherapy using body system chapter codes

When a code classifying radiotherapy is available within a body system chapter this must be sequenced before a code from category **X65 Radiotherapy delivery**. ***See PCSX20: Radiotherapy (X65, X67–X68).***

Approach to organ (Y46–Y52 and Y74-Y76)

See PCSY6: Approach to organ (Y46–Y52 and Y74-Y76)

Approach to organ under image control (Y53 and Y78)

See PCSY7: Approach to organ under image control (Y53 and Y78)

Site codes

See PCSZ1: Site codes

Laterality of operation (Z94)

See PCSZ2: Laterality of operation (Z94)

CHAPTER A
Nervous System
(A01–A84)

Coding standards and guidance

PCSA1: Guide tube anterior cingulotomy (A03.1)

The following codes and sequencing must be used for a guide tube anterior cingulotomy when performed using radiofrequency energy under magnetic resonance image control:

A03.1	**Stereotactic leucotomy**
Y47.-	**Burrhole approach to contents of cranium**
Y11.4	**Radiofrequency controlled thermal destruction of organ NOC**
Y53.7	**Approach to organ under magnetic resonance imaging control**
Z01.7	**Cingulate gyrus**

PCSA2: Pain relief procedures

Procedure		OPCS-4 code(s)
Block, brachial plexus		A73.5 + Z08.9
Block, caudal	- long acting pain relief	A52.2
	- destructive	A54.1
Block, cervical plexus	- long acting pain relief	A73.5
	- destructive	A60.5
Block, coeliac plexus	- long acting pain relief	A81.2
	- destructive, chemical	A76.5
	- destructive, cryotherapy	A77.5
	- destructive, radiofrequency	A78.5
	- destructive NEC	A79.5
Block, dorsal root ganglion nerve	- destructive NEC	A57.5 + Z07.-
	- destructive, radiofrequency	A57.3 + Z07.-
	- destructive, chemical	A57.4 + Z07.-
Block, facet joint		V54.4 + V55.-
Block, guanethidine	- long acting pain relief	A81.2
	- destructive	A76.-
Block, intercostal nerve	- long acting pain relief	A73.5 + Z07.2
Block, peripheral nerve root	- pain relief	A73.5 + site
Block, pudendal	- long acting pain relief	A73.5 + Z11.3

PCSA2: *continued*

Block/blockade, stellate ganglion	- long acting pain relief	**A81.1**
	- destructive, chemical	**A76.8 + Z92.3**
	- destructive, cryotherapy	**A77.8 + Z92.3**
	- destructive, radiofrequency	**A78.8 + Z92.3**
	- destructive	**A79.8 + Z92.3**
Block, sympathetic nerve	- long acting pain relief	**A81.2 + site**
	- destructive, chemical	**A76.-**
	- destructive, cryotherapy	**A77.-**
	- destructive, radiofrequency	**A78.-**
	- destructive NEC	**A79.-**
Block, trigeminal nerve	- long acting pain relief	**A36.5**
	- destructive	**A26.3**
Cryoprobe peripheral nerve lesion		**A61.2 + site**
Denervation, trigeminal nerve	- pain relief	**A36.5**
	- destructive	**A26.3**
Destruction spinal nerve, radiofrequency controlled, thermal		**A57.3**
Epidural, for pain relief	- dorsal, cervical, thoracic	**A52.8 + Z06.-**
	- lumbar	**A52.1**
	- sacral	**A52.2**
Intrathecal pump	- implant	**A54.3**
	- refilling	**A54.4 + Y03.1**
	- removal	**A54.5**
Neurodestruction	- peripheral nerve	**A60.5 + site**
	- sympathetic nerve	**A76.-**
Stimulator/neurostimulator dorsal column		**A48.3 + Z06.2**

PCSA3: Neurostimulators (A09, A33, A48 and A70)

When a neurostimulator is permanently implanted under the skin the following codes and sequencing are applied:

- Code that classifies the implantation, introduction or insertion of neurostimulator
- Chapter Z site code, where this adds additional information

PCSA3: *continued*

When electrode leads are implanted temporarily to test whether the intervention is likely to be effective and the pulse generator device is not implanted under the skin the following codes and sequencing are applied:

- Code that classifies insertion of neurostimulator electrodes

- **Y70.5 Temporary operations**

- Chapter Z site code, where this add further information

- **Z94.- laterality of operation** (if applicable)

Example:

Temporary insertion of neurostimulator electrodes into the right sacral nerve.

A70.4	**Insertion of neurostimulator electrodes into peripheral nerve**
Y70.5	**Temporary operations**
Z11.2	**Sacral nerve**
Z94.2	**Right sided operation**

Transcutaneous stimulation of the cervical branch of the vagus nerve:

A70.7	**Application of transcutaneous electrical nerve stimulator**
Z04.4	**Vagus nerve (x)**

PCSA4: Cortical mapping (A11.4)

Cortical mapping can take several hours over a number of days. It must only be coded once per hospital provider spell as follows:

- Assign the following codes according to the type of electrodes that have been placed:

A11.1	**Placement of depth electrodes for electroencephalography**
Y47.-	**Burrhole approach to contents of cranium** (if performed using this approach)

  or

A11.2	**Placement of surface electrodes for electroencephalography**
Y46.-	**Open approach to contents of cranium** (if performed using this approach)

- Assign code **A11.4 Cortical mapping** directly afterwards.

PCSA5: Electroconvulsive therapy (A83)

Each individual treatment within a course of electroconvulsive therapy (ECT) must be recorded separately.

- For the first administration within a course of therapy assign code **A83.8 Other specified electroconvulsive therapy** in the primary position

  o Where a number of courses have been administered during the same consultant episode, all instances of **A83.8** must be assigned before assigning **A83.9**

- For subsequent administrations in the same course of therapy (whether in the same consultant episode within a hospital provider spell or a subsequent hospital provider spell) code **A83.9 Unspecified electroconvulsive therapy** must be assigned.

Patients undergoing ECT are usually given a course of therapy which involves a number of treatments. Subsequent treatments within a course may be given during the same hospital provider spell as the first treatment or during a subsequent hospital provider spell(s).

Examples:

Administration of first treatment in a course of electroconvulsive therapy. Second and third treatments administered within the same hospital provider spell.

A83.8	**Other specified electroconvulsive therapy**
A83.9	**Unspecified electroconvulsive therapy**
A83.9	**Unspecified electroconvulsive therapy**

Administration of fourth treatment in a course of electroconvulsive therapy.

A83.9	**Unspecified electroconvulsive therapy**

Administration of two courses of ECT, each course consisting of two treatments during one consultant episode.

A83.8	**Other specified electroconvulsive therapy**
A83.8	**Other specified electroconvulsive therapy**
A83.9	**Unspecified electroconvulsive therapy**
A83.9	**Unspecified electroconvulsive therapy**

Standard EEG (**A84.1 Electroencephalography NEC**) is usually performed in outpatients and can last up to about an hour. It uses simultaneous video to allow the reporting clinician to visualise any attacks or seizures occurring during the test. ***See also PCSU5: Diagnostic tests (U22–U33 and U40) for guidance on Electroencephalograph telemetry (U22.1).***

PCSA7: Repair of spinal dura (A51.8)

Repair of the spinal dura (as opposed to the dura of the brain) must be coded using **A51.8 Other specified other operations on meninges of spinal cord.**

An additional code(s) from **Chapter Y Subsidiary classification of methods of operation** must also be assigned to specify the type of repair where this adds further information and the information is documented within the medical record.

Codes within the range **A38-A43** must not be used to classify procedures on the spinal dura, as these categories classify procedures on the <u>meninges of the brain</u> only.

PCSA6: Evoked potential recording (A84.4)

A84.4 Evoked potential recording must be coded whenever it has been documented to have been carried out.

Code **A84.7 Sleep studies NEC** includes a '*full polysomnography*'. A full polysomnography will include electroencephalography (EEG), electrooculography (EOG), and surface electromyography (EMG), together with multiple sleep latency tests (MSLT) and the maintenance of wakefulness tests (MWT). These are carried out by specialists in Neurosciences and the emphasis will be on the diagnosis of disorders of sleep pattern without any disorder of breathing. ***See also Chapter U for guidance on polysomnography (U33.1).***

CHAPTER B
Endocrine System and Breast
(B01–B41)

Chapter standards and guidance

Operations on the skin of the breast are classified to Chapter S. The skin of the nipple and areola, however, are classified to this chapter.

Coding standards and guidance

PCSB1: Pituitary excision with skull based reconstruction

When pituitary excision (partial or total) is performed using endonasal endoscopic trans-sphenoidal approach, and an anterior skull based reconstruction is performed (the defect created in the anterior skull base by the approach is closed using a mucosal flap), the following codes and sequencing must be assigned in addition to the code(s) for the pituitary excision:

E15.8	Other specified operations on sphenoid sinus
Y76.6	Endonasal endoscopic approach to other body cavity
Y26.1	Reconstruction of organ NOC
S28.8	Other specified flap of mucosa
Y76.6	Endonasal endoscopic approach to other body cavity

See *PGCS1: Endoscopic and minimal access operations that do not have a specific code.*

Example:

Hypophysectomy and anterior skull based reconstruction with mucosal flap. All performed using endonasal endoscopic trans-sphenoidal approach.

B01.2	Trans-sphenoidal hypophysectomy
Y76.6	Endonasal endoscopic approach to other body cavity
E15.8	Other specified operations on sphenoid sinus
Y76.6	Endonasal endoscopic approach to other body cavity
Y26.1	Reconstruction of organ NOC
S28.8	Other specified flap of mucosa
Y76.6	Endonasal endoscopic approach to other body cavity

Parathyroid washout (B16.4)

B16.4 Parathyroid washout is a nuclear medicine imaging procedure and a code from categories **Y93, Y94, Y97** and **Y98** must not be assigned in addition.

See PCSU3: Nuclear medicine imaging procedures.

PCSB2: Excision of breast with lymph node clearance and breast reconstruction (B27-B29, B38, B39 and B41)

When a procedure classifiable to categories **B27 Total excision of breast, B28 Other excision of breast** or **B41 Excision of breast** is performed with an axilliary lymph node clearance and breast reconstruction, the code from category **B27, B28** or **B41** must be coded first, immediately followed by the lymph node clearance, followed by code(s) for the breast reconstruction (**B29, B38** or **B39**.)

Eye
(C01–C90)

Coding standards and guidance

PCSC1: Local anaesthetic for ophthalmology procedures (C90)

Codes in category **C90 Local anaesthetic for ophthalmology procedures** must only be assigned in a secondary position.

These codes are available for Trusts that wish to collect this data for local purposes. With the exception of radiotherapy performed under general anaesthetic, there is **no** mandatory requirement to code anaesthetics.

See also:

- *PCSX20: Radiotherapy (X65, X67–X68)*

- *PCSY10: Anaesthetic (Y80–Y84).*

CHAPTER D
Ear
(D01–D28)

Coding standards and guidance

PCSD1: Attachment of bone anchored hearing prosthesis (D13)

Codes **D13.1 First stage insertion of fixtures for bone anchored hearing prosthesis**, D13.2 **Second stage insertion of fixtures for bone anchored hearing prosthesis** and **D13.5 One stage insertion of fixtures for bone anchored hearing prosthesis** do not include the fitting of the bone anchored hearing aid itself.

The fitting of a bone anchored hearing aid must be coded separately using **D13.6 Fitting of external hearing prosthesis to bone anchored fixtures.**

In most cases, the hearing aid is inserted during an outpatient appointment.

PCSD3: Combined approach tympanoplasty (D14.4)

A code for the graft material used must not be assigned in addition to code **D14.4 Combined approach tympanoplasty** as the graft is implicit within the code.

PCSD2: Replacement of the ossicular chain (D16.8)

When coding a graft replacement of the ossicular chain using a combination of bone plate, fibrin glue and cartilage, code **D16.8 Other specified reconstruction of ossicular chain** must be assigned.

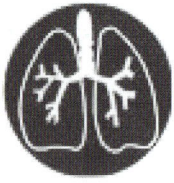

CHAPTER E
Respiratory Tract
(E01–E98)

Coding standards and guidance

Pituitary excision with skull based reconstruction

See PCSB1: Pituitary excision with skull based reconstruction.

PCSE1: Laryngopharyngectomy (E19 and E29)

When coding laryngopharyngectomy the following codes and sequencing must be used:

E19	**Pharyngectomy**
E29	**Excision of larynx**

The fourth character codes assigned will be dependent upon whether the excisions are total, partial or unspecified.

Examples:

Laryngopharyngectomy

E19.2   **Partial pharyngectomy**
Includes: *Pharyngectomy NEC*
E29.6   **Laryngectomy NEC**

Partial vertical laryngectomy and total pharyngectomy

E19.1   **Total pharyngectomy**
E29.3   **Partial vertical laryngectomy**

PCSE2: Diagnostic fibreoptic endoscopic examination of lower respiratory tract (E49)

When bronchoscopy is performed with washings, brushings or biopsy the following codes must be used:

Bronchoscopy with washings:

E49.2   **Diagnostic fibreoptic endoscopic examination of lower respiratory tract and lavage of lesion of lower respiratory tract**

Bronchoscopy with brushings:

E49.3   **Diagnostic fibreoptic endoscopic examination of lower respiratory tract and brush cytology of lesion of lower respiratory tract**

Bronchoscopy with brushings and washings:

E49.4   **Diagnostic fibreoptic endoscopic examination of lower respiratory tract with lavage and brush cytology of lesion of lower respiratory tract**

Bronchoscopy with biopsy, brushings and washings:

E49.5   **Diagnostic fibreoptic endoscopic examination of lower respiratory tract with biopsy, lavage and brush cytology of lesion of lower respiratory tract**

PCSE2: *continued*

Bronchoscopy with biopsy and brushings:

E49.1   **Diagnostic fibreoptic endoscopic examination of lower respiratory tract and biopsy of lesion of lower respiratory tract**

Y21.1   **Brush cytology or organ NOC**

Bronchoscopy with biopsy and washings:

E49.1   **Diagnostic fibreoptic endoscopic examination of lower respiratory tract and biopsy of lesion of lower respiratory tract**

Y21.8   **Other specified cytology of organ NOC**

PCSE3: Endobronchial-ultrasound guided transbronchial needle aspiration (E63.2)

Endobronchial ultrasound-guided transbronchial needle aspiration (EBUS-TBNA) must be coded using the following codes and sequencing:

E63.2   **Endobronchial ultrasound examination of mediastinum**

Y20.-   **Biopsy of organ NOC**

Updated ✱

PCSE4: Non operations on lower respiratory tract (E85–E98) and ventilation support (E85)

Codes in categories **E85–E98** must only to be used for outpatient coding, or if the patient is admitted solely for the purpose of a procedure/intervention.

The exception to this standard is category **E85 Ventilation support**. Codes within this category must always be assigned when ventilation support is performed in either an inpatient or outpatient setting.

PCSE5: Invasive ventilation with tracheostomy (E85.1)

When a tracheostomy is performed for invasive ventilation the following codes and sequencing must be applied:

E85.1   **Invasive ventilation**

E42.3   **Temporary tracheostomy**

+ PCSE6: Nasendoscopy.

CHAPTER G
Upper Digestive Tract
(G01–G82)

Chapter standards and guidance

PChSG1: Failed intubation at upper gastrointestinal tract endoscopy

When a patient is admitted for a gastrointestinal tract endoscopy and the patient is unable to tolerate the scope and statements such as 'failed intubation' is documented in the medical record; the procedure must not be coded unless the point of abandonment is beyond the mouth.

See PGCS3: Incomplete, unfinished, abandoned and failed procedures.

If the point of abandonment of the procedure is no further than the mouth, or if it has not been identified, this cannot be coded using OPCS-4. However, the coder must clarify the point of abandonment with the responsible consultant if this information has not been documented in the medical record.

The appropriate ICD-10 code(s) for the condition(s) which prompted the endoscopy to be performed (e.g. gastric ulcer, epigastric pain, gastrointestinal bleed) are assigned.

Examples:

Patient with dysphagia admitted for upper GI endoscopy. Intubation failed and the scope was removed (from the pharynx) by the patient and the procedure could not be completed

> **E25.9** **Unspecified diagnostic endoscopic examination of pharynx**

> The ICD-10 code for dysphagia would also be assigned.

Patient with epigastric pain admitted for gastroscopy. The patient could not tolerate the scope in his mouth and the procedure could not be performed.

> **No OPCS-4 codes are assigned**

> The ICD-10 code for epigastric pain would be assigned.

Endoscopic ultrasound staging examination

See PCSY5: Endoscopic ultrasound staging examination of organ NOC (Y41.2) for the standards for coding an endoscopic ultrasound examination (EUS) performed as a staging examination.

Conversion procedures

See PGCS16: Conversion procedures.

Coding standards and guidance

PCSG5: Coagulation of bleeding lesion(s) of upper gastrointestinal tract (G20.1 and G46.2)

Codes **G20.1 Fibreoptic endoscopic coagulation of bleeding lesion of oesophagus** and **G46.2 Fibreoptic endoscopic coagulation of bleeding lesion of upper gastrointestinal tract** must only be assigned when coagulation of bleeding lesion(s) is performed as a therapeutic procedure. These codes must **not** be used to classify coagulation as a means of haemostasis at the end of a procedure.

PCSG1: Non-endoscopic oesophageal balloon dilation under image control (G21.4)

Oesophageal balloon dilation under image control, not using an endoscope must be coded using the following codes and sequencing:

> **G21.4** **Intubation of oesophagus NEC**
> **Y40.3** **Balloon dilation of organ NOC**
> **Y53.-** **Approach to organ under image control**

Code **G30.5 Maintenance of gastric band** also includes:

- Maintenance of gastric port
- Attention to gastric band connecting tube
- Resiting of gastric band access port
- Replacement of gastric band access port

See also PGCS17: Maintenance and attention to procedures.

PCSG2: Removal of percutaneous endoscopic gastrostomy (G34.5 and G44.7)

Non-endoscopic removal of percutaneous endoscopic gastrostomy (PEG) must be coded to:

> **G34.5** **Attention to gastrostomy tube**
> **Y03.7** **Removal of prosthesis from organ NOC.**

PCSG3: Insertion of nasogastric feeding tube (G47.8)

Insertion of a nasogastric (NG) feeding tube must only be coded when a patient is admitted **solely for the purpose of** insertion. In these instances, the following OPCS-4 code must be used:

> **G47.8** **Other specified intubation of stomach**

PCSG4: Removal or renewal of gastric balloon (G48.6)

The removal of a gastric balloon must be coded using the following codes:

> **G48.6** **Attention to gastric balloon**
> **Y03.7** **Removal of prosthesis from organ NOC**

The renewal of a gastric balloon must be coded using the following codes:

> **G48.6** **Attention to gastric balloon**
> **Y03.2** **Renewal of prosthesis in organ NOC**

CHAPTER H
Lower Digestive Tract
(H01–H70)

Chapter standards and guidance

Emergency procedures

Separate categories exist within this chapter to classify emergency procedures. *See PGCS15: Emergency procedures.*

Coding standards and guidance

PCSH1: Closure or reversal of Hartmann's procedure (H15.4)

The following codes must be assigned for reversal or closure of Hartmann's procedure:

H15.4	**Closure of colostomy**	
Y16.2	**Anastomosis of organ NOC**	
Z29.1	**Rectum**	

PCSH2: Colonoscopy with ileal intubation (H22.1)

A colonoscopy with ileal intubation and biopsy of the terminal ileum is classified using the following codes and sequencing:

H22.1	**Diagnostic fibreoptic endoscopic examination of colon and biopsy of lesion of colon**
Z27.6	**Ileum**

A code from category **G80.- Diagnostic endoscopic examination of ileum** must only be assigned if it is specifically documented in the medical record that the patient had a diagnostic ileoscopy or a diagnostic endoscopic examination of the ileum.

PCSH3: Banding of haemorrhoids during endoscopic procedures (H52.4)

When banding of haemorrhoids is carried out in conjunction with an endoscopic procedure, both **H52.4 Rubber band ligation of haemorrhoid** and the OPCS-4 endoscopic procedure code must be assigned.

Example:

Sigmoidoscopy and biopsy of sigmoid colon with banding of haemorrhoids

H52.4	**Rubber band ligation of haemorrhoid**
H25.1	**Diagnostic endoscopic examination of lower bowel and biopsy of lesion of lower bowel using fibreoptic sigmoidoscope**
Z28.6	**Sigmoid colon**

PCSH4: Antegrade colonic enema (H62.5)

The following codes must be assigned for antegrade colonic enema:

H62.5	**Irrigation of bowel NEC**
Y51.5	**Approach to organ through appendicostomy**

Haemorrhoidal artery ligation (L70.3)

For the standard for coding Haemorrhoidal artery ligation (HALO). *See PCSL2: Haemorrhoidal artery ligation (L70.3).*

Other Abdominal Organs – Principally Digestive
(J01–J77)

Chapter Standards and guidance

Endoscopic ultrasound staging examination

See PCSY5: Endoscopic ultrasound staging examination of organ NOC (Y41.2) for the standards for coding an endoscopic ultrasound examination (EUS) performed as a staging examination.

Coding standards and guidance

Endoscopic retrograde cholangiopancreatography standard exception

If a diagnostic endoscopic procedure proceeds to a therapeutic endoscopic procedure on the same site during the same theatre visit, only the therapeutic procedure is coded (See *PGCS10 Coding endoscopic procedures*). An exception to this standard is endoscopic retrograde cholangiopancreatography (ERCP) performed concurrently with a therapeutic endoscopic procedure as indicated by the notes at the appropriate codes within the Tabular list.

PCSJ1: Selective internal radiotherapy (SIRT) of liver using microspheres (J12.3)

Selective internal radiotherapy (SIRT) of liver using microspheres under image control must be coded using the following codes and sequencing:

J12.3	**Selective internal radiotherapy with microspheres to lesion of liver**
X65.3	**Delivery of a fraction of interstitial radiotherapy**
Y36.4	**Introduction of non-removable radioactive substance into organ for brachytherapy NOC**
Y89.-	**Brachytherapy** (where necessary)
Y53.-	**Approach to organ under image control**

See also PCSX20: Radiotherapy (X65, X67–X68).

PCSJ2: Failed or abandoned endoscopic retrograde cholangiopancreatography (J43.9)

A failed or abandoned ERCP, (i.e. an ERCP with incomplete insertion of the endoscope, or complete insertion of the endoscope but the ampulla cannot be cannulated) must be coded as **J43.9 Unspecified diagnostic endoscopic retrograde examination of bile duct and pancreatic duct**. This is the exception to the coding standard for failed procedures (See *PGCS3: Incomplete, unfinished, abandoned and failed procedures*).

PCSJ3: Cholecystectomy with endoscopic retrograde cholangiopancreatography

When endoscopic retrograde cholangiopancreatography (ERCP) is performed at the same time as cholecystectomy, the ERCP must be coded in a secondary position.

CHAPTER K
Heart
(K01–K78)

Chapter standards and guidance

Approach to organ under image control (Y53 and Y78)

Many procedures within this chapter are performed using arteriotomy approach and/or image control, see **PCSY7: Approach to organ under image control (Y53 and Y78)** for the standards for the use of codes in categories **Y53** and **Y78**.

Cardiopulmonary bypass (Y73.1)

Procedures in this chapter may be performed using cardiopulmonary bypass, for the standards for coding **Y73.1 Cardiopulmonary bypass** *see PCSY8: Cardiopulmonary bypass (Y73.1)*.

Coding standards and guidance

PCSK1: Transcatheter aortic valve implantation (K26)

For transcatheter aortic valve implantation (TAVI) using a surgical approach through left ventricle (transapical or transventricular approach) assign the following codes:

K26.-	**Plastic repair of aortic valve**
Y49.4	**Transapical approach to heart**

For TAVI using a transluminal approach through an artery (i.e. femoral, subclavian, axillary or aorta) assign the following codes:

K26.-	**Plastic repair of aortic valve**
Y79.-	**Approach to organ through artery**
Y53.-	**Approach to organ under image control**

PCSK2: Insertion of a combination of coronary artery stents

When a combination of drug-eluting and metal or plastic stents have been inserted during a coronary artery procedure the following codes and sequencing must be used:

- body system chapter code describing the insertion of the drug-eluting stent

- a code from category **Y14 Placement of stent in organ NOC** to classify the insertion of the other types of coronary stent(s)

- a code from category **Y53.- Approach to organ under image control** to classify the method of image control used.

Example:

Percutaneous coronary balloon angioplasty and insertion of two drug-eluting stents and one expanding metal stent into coronary artery using image control

K75.1	**Percutaneous transluminal balloon angioplasty and insertion of 1–2 drug-eluting stents into coronary artery**
Y14.2	**Insertion of expanding metal stent into organ NOC**
Y53.9	**Unspecified approach to organ under image control**

PCSK3: Coronary arteriography with fractional flow reserve measurement or pressure wire studies and coronary angioplasty using fractional flow reserve

When measurement of Fractional Flow Reserve (FFR), or pressure wire studies is performed at the same time as coronary arteriography, the following codes and sequencing must be used:

K63.4- K63.6 Coronary arteriography
K51.8 Other specified diagnostic transluminal operations on coronary artery
Y44.2 Monitoring of pressure in organ NOC
Y53.- Approach to organ under image control

When coronary angioplasty and/or insertion of stent(s) into the coronary artery/arteries are performed using FFR the following codes and sequencing must be used:

Code classifying angioplasty and/or insertion of stent

Y14 Placement of stent in organ NOC (when a combination of stents have been inserted)
Y44.2 Monitoring of pressure in organ NOC
Y53.- Approach to organ under image control

Examples:

Coronary arteriography using one catheter and fractional flow reserve (pressure wire studies) under percutaneous image control

K63.5 Coronary arteriography using single catheter
K51.8 Other specified diagnostic transluminal operations on coronary artery
Y44.2 Monitoring of pressure in organ NOC
Y53.9 Unspecified approach to organ under image control

Percutaneous coronary balloon angioplasty and insertion of two drug-eluting stents and one expanding metal stent into coronary artery using FFR guidance under fluoroscopic image control

K75.1 Percutaneous transluminal balloon angioplasty and insertion of 1-2 drug eluting stents into coronary artery
Y14.2 Insertion of expanding metal stent into organ NOC
Y44.2 Monitoring of pressure in organ NOC
Y53.4 Approach to organ under fluoroscopic control

PCSK4: Coronary angioplasty and insertion of coronary stents using intravascular ultrasound guidance

When coronary angioplasty and/or insertion of stent(s) into the coronary artery(s) are performed using intravascular ultrasound guidance (IVUS) the following codes and sequencing must be used:

Code classifying angioplasty and/or insertion of stent

Y14.- Placement of stent in organ NOC (when a combination of stents have been inserted)
Y53.2 Approach to organ under ultrasonic control (to identify IVUS)
Y53.- Approach to organ under image control (where the method of image control is not ultrasound)

Example:

Percutaneous transluminal balloon angioplasty of multiple coronary arteries using IVUS guidance under fluoroscopic image control

K49.2 Percutaneous transluminal balloon angioplasty of multiple coronary arteries
Y53.2 Approach to organ under ultrasonic control
Y53.4 Approach to organ under fluoroscopic control

PCSK5: Insertion of ventricular assist device (K54 and K56)

For the insertion of a ventricular assist device (VAD) using an open approach assign the following codes:

K54.-   **Open heart assist operations**
Y70.5   **Temporary operations**

For the insertion of a ventricular assist device (VAD) using a percutaneous approach assign the following codes:

K56.2   **Transluminal insertion of heart assist system NEC**
Y53.-   **Approach to organ under image control** (if image control is used)
Y70.5   **Temporary operations**

PCSK6: Ablation of the heart with 3D mapping (K58.6)

3D mapping of the heart is an inherent part of ablation of the conducting system of the heart and is rarely performed on its own, therefore code **K58.6 Percutaneous transluminal three dimensional electroanatomic mapping of conducting system of heart** must not be assigned in addition to an ablation code from categories **K57 Other therapeutic transluminal operations on heart** or **K62 Therapeutic transluminal operations on heart**.

PCSK7: Implantation and renewal of cardiac resynchronisation therapy defibrillator (K59.6 and K59.7)

Implantation or renewal of a cardiac resynchronisation therapy defibrillator (CRT-D) device using either **two or three** leads is coded to **K59.6 Implantation of cardioverter defibrillator using three electrode leads** or **K59.7 Renewal of cardioverter defibrillator using three electrode leads**.

Evaluation of cardioverter defibrillator (X50.5)

See PCSX15: Evaluation of cardioverter defibrillator (X50.5)

PCSK8: Angiocardiography (ventriculography) of the heart and coronary arteriography (K63)

When an angiocardiography (ventriculography) of the heart (codes **K63.1–K63.3**) is performed with a coronary arteriography (codes **K63.4–K63.6**), during the same radiology/theatre visit, both procedures must be recorded. A code from category **Y53.- Approach to organ under image control** must also be assigned in a secondary position in order to classify the method of image control used.

A code from category **K65 Catheterisation of heart** must not be assigned in addition to codes in category **K63 Contrast radiology of heart** as catheterisation is implicit within these codes.

Examples:

Coronary arteriography using two catheters performed during the same radiology/theatre visit with a left ventriculography under percutaneous image control

K63.3   **Angiocardiography of left side of heart NEC**
K63.4   **Coronary arteriography using two catheters**
Y53.9   **Unspecified approach to organ under image control**

Cardiac catheterisation with angiocardiography of right and left side of heart using image control

K63.1   **Angiocardiography of combination of right and left side of heart**
Y53.9   **Unspecified approach to organ under image control**

CHAPTER L
Arteries and Veins
(L01–L99, O01–O05, O15, O20)

Chapter standards and guidance

Procedures carried out on coronary blood vessels are excluded from this Chapter and are classified in Chapter K Heart instead.

Certain specific blood vessels are excluded from this chapter and are classified in other body system chapters, e.g. ligation of maxillary artery using sublabial approach is coded to **E12.1**.

Approach to organ under image control (Y53 and Y78)

Many procedures within this chapter are performed using arteriotomy approach and/or image control, **see PCSY7: Approach to organ under image control (Y53 and Y78)** for the standards for the use of codes in categories **Y53** and **Y78**.

Emergency procedures

Separate categories exist within this chapter to classify emergency procedures. See **PGCS15: Emergency procedures.**

Cardiopulmonary bypass (Y73.1)

Procedures in this chapter may be performed using cardiopulmonary bypass, for the standards for coding **Y73.1 Cardiopulmonary bypass** see **PCSY8: Cardiopulmonary bypass (Y73.1)**.

PChSL1: Interventions not specifically classifiable within a named artery category

Codes in categories **L65–L72** must not be used when an intervention is classifiable within a named artery category from the range **L01–L63**.

Codes within principal category **L71 Therapeutic transluminal operations on other artery** and extended category **L66 Other therapeutic transluminal operations on artery** must be used to code interventions not classifiable at fourth-character level within named artery categories. A site code from Chapter Z must also be assigned.

For 'other specified' and 'unspecified' procedures on named arteries that cannot be classified at specific fourth-characters within categories **L66** and **L71**, the .8 and .9 subcategories at named artery categories, e.g. **L63.8**, **L63.9** etc. must be used instead.

Example:

Percutaneous transluminal atherectomy of common femoral artery under image control

> **L71.7** **Percutaneous transluminal atherectomy**
> *Note: Use a subsidiary code to identify method of image control (Y53)*
> **Y53.9** **Unspecified approach to organ under image control**
> **Z38.3** **Common femoral artery**

Although this procedure is on the femoral artery which appears at a number of categories as a named artery (**L56–L63**), a code does not exist which classifies percutaneous atherectomy of the femoral artery within this range, therefore as a code is available at category **L71**, it must be classified here together with a site code from Chapter Z to identify the specific artery.

PChSL2: Assigning codes for specifically classifiable arteries

Only when an artery or its branches is specified in the category/code description or at the category inclusions can these codes be assigned. A site code must be assigned in addition when the artery is listed as an inclusion term.

Where the artery is not specifically referred to within the code description or inclusion, even if the origin is known, do **not** assign a code from these categories. A code from categories **L65–L72** must be used instead with the addition of a site code from Chapter Z where available.

Due to the vast number of arteries in the human body, it is not possible to allocate categories for specific operations on every named artery, down to the smallest branch. Specific categories are available in Chapter L for the major branches of the aorta and specified tributaries which are included within each as inclusion terms where appropriate.

This allows the classification of a major part of arterial surgery into a relatively small number of discrete anatomical groups. This specification does not extend beyond the actual named vessels.

Examples:

Ligation of axillary artery

> **L38.2**   **Ligation of subclavian artery**
> *Includes:*   *Axillary artery*
> *Brachial artery*
> *Vertebral artery*
>
> **Z36.3**   **Axillary artery**

Ligation of splenic artery

> **L70.3**   **Ligation of artery NEC**
> **Z37.7**   **Splenic artery**

PChSL3: Insertion of stents and stent grafts

There are a number of dedicated codes that classify the insertion of stents on various sites within Chapter L. These codes must be supplemented by a code from categories **L76**, **L89** or **O20**, to indicate the type and number of stents or stent grafts inserted, as indicated by the **Notes** at category or code level.

When a stent has been inserted and the number and type of stent is unknown, the default code is **L76.9 Unspecified endovascular placement of stent**.

When a stent graft has been inserted and the number and type of stent is unknown, the default code is **O20.9 Unspecified endovascular placement of stent graft**.

When angioplasty and insertion of stent or stent graft are performed at the same time and individual codes are available for the angioplasty and for the stent/stent graft insertion, only the code for the stent/stent graft insertion is required, because the angioplasty is implicit within the stent/stent graft insertion code.

Examples:

Percutaneous transluminal balloon angioplasty of pulmonary artery and insertion of one metallic stent under ultrasonic control

> **L13.6**   **Percutaneous transluminal insertion of stent into pulmonary artery**
> *Note: Use a supplementary code for placement of stent (L76, L89, O20)*
> *Note: Use a subsidiary code to identify method of image control (Y53)*
>
> **L76.1**   **Endovascular placement of one metallic stent**
> **Y53.2**   **Approach to organ under ultrasonic control**

Insertion of two endovascular stent grafts into thoracic aortic aneurysm using femoral arteriotomy approach under ultrasonic guidance

> **L27.3** **Endovascular insertion of stent graft for thoracic aortic aneurysm**
>> *Note: Use a subsidiary code to identify arteriotomy approach to organ under image control (Y78)*
>> *Note: Use a supplementary code for placement of stent (O20)*
>
> **O20.4** **Endovascular placement of two stent grafts**
> **Y78.3** **Arteriotomy approach to organ using image guidance with ultrasound**

PChSL4: Removal of bypass grafts

The removal of bypass grafts must be coded to the original operation bypass category with the fourth-character **.8** plus code **Y26.4 Removal of other repair material from organ NOC** unless there is a specific fourth-character code that classifies removal of the bypass graft.

Example:

Removal of femoral bypass graft

> **L59.8** **Other specified other bypass of femoral artery**
> **Y26.4** **Removal of other repair material from organ NOC**

Coding standards and guidance

Category **L04** classifies procedures on *both* pulmonary arteries, so it is not necessary to add code **Z94.1** to indicate a bilateral operation.

PCSL1: Anastomosis without a site specific code (L16-L28 and L48-L63)

Anastomotic sites that are not specifically indicated at the fourth-character level within categories **L16–L28** and **L48–L63** must be assigned to the **.8** within the relevant category.

Example:

Bypass of segment of aorta by anastomosis of aorta to common femoral artery

> **L21.8** **Other specified other bypass of segment of aorta**

PCSL8: Replacement/repair of aorta for aortic aneurysm and aortic dissection (L18-L21, L27-L28)

When multiple segments of the aorta are replaced/repaired and the individual segments are classifiable to different four character codes, each segment replaced/repaired must be coded separately.

The replacement of the aortic arch must be classified to a code for the replacement of thoracic segment of the aorta, followed by **Z34.2 Aortic arch** to further specify the particular section of the thoracic aorta.

The replacement/repair of a juxtarenal abdominal aortic aneurysm/dissection has an increased level of surgical and postoperative complexity, and must be assigned the appropriate code for the replacement/repair of a suprarenal aortic aneurysm/dissection.

The open replacement of the aorta for an aortic dissection without aneurysm must be classified to categories **L20 Other emergency bypass of segment of aorta** <u>OR</u> **L21 Other bypass of segment of aorta**.

When a Frozen Elephant Trunk (FET) procedure has been performed, this must be classified using the appropriate open replacement/repair code from categories **L18 – L21** and a supplementary code from **O20 Endovascular placement of stent graft**.

See also PGCS15: Emergency procedures.

A Frozen Elephant Trunk (FET) is a single-stage hybrid procedure, combining a conventional open approach with endovascular techniques to treat extensive aortic aneurysms or aortic dissections.

Bare metal stents (without covering material) are not used in endovascular aortic aneurysm repair therefore where only 'stent' (bare metal stent) and not 'stent-graft' (stent with material covering) is documented in the medical record the coder should check to see if, in fact, a stent graft has been used and assign a code from category **L27 Transluminal insertion of stent graft for aneurysmal segment of aorta**.

PCSL2: Haemorrhoidal artery ligation (L70.3)

Haemorrhoidal artery ligation (HALO) is an ultrasound guided procedure, performed on the arteries supplying blood to the haemorrhoids, rather than on the haemorrhoids themselves, therefore the following codes must be used to classify this procedure:

L70.3	Ligation of artery NEC
Y53.2	Approach to organ under ultrasonic control
Z37.8	Specified lateral branch of abdominal aorta NEC

PCSL3: Embolisation of uterine fibroids (L71.3)

Embolisation of uterine fibroids is performed under image control on the uterine artery which supplies blood to the fibroids. Therefore the following codes must be used to classify this procedure:

L71.3	Percutaneous transluminal embolisation of artery
Y53.-	Approach to organ under image control
Z96.6	Uterine artery
Z94.-	Laterality of operation

As code **L73.1 Mechanical embolic protection NEC** would only be used to denote a mechanical embolic protection which is *not* covered more precisely by any other code, e.g. **L73.2 Mechanical embolic protection of artery**, it is expected that codes **L73.8** and **L73.9** would not be used. To maintain the integrity of the classification these codes are included.

PCSL4: Fistuloplasty of arteriovenous fistula (L74.3)

Fistuloplasty of an arteriovenous fistula is coded using the following codes and sequencing:

L74.3 **Attention to arteriovenous shunt**
Y40.- **Dilation of organ NOC**
Y53.- **Approach to organ under image control** (if image control is used)
Z site code (when the site is stated)
Z94.- **Laterality**

PCSL5: Varicose vein operations (L84, L85 and L87)

Codes from category **L84 Combined operations on varicose vein of leg** must be used when any **ligation**, **stripping** or **avulsion** of varicose veins of leg, described in categories **L85 Ligation of varicose vein of leg** and **L87 Other operations on varicose vein of leg**, are performed at the same time.

Example:

Stripping and avulsion of right recurrent long saphenous vein

L84.4 **Combined operations on recurrent long saphenous vein**
Z94.2 **Right sided operation**

PCSL6: Insertion of vascular closure device (L97.6)

Code **L97.6 Insertion of vascular closure device** must not be assigned when it was applied as part of a main procedure to close and seal the arteries. **L97.6 Insertion of vascular closure device** must only be assigned when this was the only procedure that took place.

PCSL7: Aneurysm sizes (O01)

The sizes of aneurysms described at category **O01 Transluminal coil embolisation of aneurysm of artery** are as follows:

- Small   = 5mm or less

- Medium   = 6mm–10mm

- Large   = 11mm–20mm

- Giant   = greater than 20mm.

CHAPTER M
Urinary
(M01–M86)

Coding standards and guidance

PCSM1: Percutaneous drainage of kidney (M13.2)

Code **M13.2 Percutaneous drainage of kidney** includes the insertion of a nephrostomy tube for drainage. The insertion of the nephrostomy tube must not be coded in addition.

PCSM2: Insertion and change of ureteric stents

Code **M29.2 Endoscopic insertion of tubal prosthesis into ureter NEC** must be used to classify the insertion of a ureteric, 'DJ' or 'JJ' stent.

The codes assigned to indicate the change of a ureteric stent depend on the type of endoscope used:

    M29.5   **Endoscopic renewal of tubal prosthesis into ureter**

    or

    M27.8   **Other specified therapeutic ureteroscopic operations on ureter**

    Y15.2   **Renewal of stent in organ NOC**

PCSM3: Extracorporeal shockwave lithotripsy of calculus of ureter (M31.1)

Cystoscopy and/or the insertion of a stent must not be coded in addition to **M31.1 Extracorporeal shockwave lithotripsy of calculus of ureter**, as these are integral parts of the procedure. A code from **Y53 Approach to organ under image control** must be assigned in addition.

However, if the stent is left in situ following the lithotripsy in order to facilitate the passage of fragments of the calculus, then the stent insertion would require coding in addition to **M31.1**, with a code from **Y14 Placement of stent in organ NOC**, as appropriate.

PCSM4: Cystoscopy with cystodiathermy and biopsy of the bladder lesion (M42.2)

Cystoscopy with cystodiathermy and biopsy of lesion of the bladder must be coded using the following codes and sequencing:

    M42.2   **Endoscopic cauterisation of lesion of bladder**

    Y20.3   **Biopsy of lesion of organ NOC**

    Site code of biopsy from Chapter Z (If the site can be further specified: i.e. the site is not just "the bladder", but is, for instance, **Z42.3 Outlet of bladder**.

PCSM5: Fluorescence cystoscopy and cystoscopy using photodynamic substance

Fluorescence cystoscopy and cystoscopy using a photodynamic substance are coded as follows:

- Body system chapter code to classify the cystoscopy

- **Y37.1 Introduction of photodynamic substance into organ NOC**

PCSM6: Catheterisation of the bladder (M47)

Urethral catheterisation (**M47.9 Unspecified urethral catheterisation of bladder**) must **not** be coded when:

- catheter insertion is performed routinely as part of, or following, a procedure
- catheter insertion is performed to keep the patient comfortable during admission, for example in an elderly immobile long stay patient.

    Neither must subsequent removal of the catheter be coded in these instances.

If a patient is catheterised for urinary retention (which may have been present on admission or developed during the admission) the insertion of the urethral catheter and its subsequent removal would **not** be considered a routine part of care and both the insertion and removal of the catheter must be coded.

If a urethral catheter is inserted routinely, but following removal the patient is unable to void urine, this indicates that the patient is in urinary retention. The reinsertion of the urethral catheter, and its subsequent removal following reinsertion, would **not** be considered a routine part of care and both the reinsertion and subsequent removal of the catheter must be coded.

When a patient is admitted for removal of an indwelling urinary catheter or trial without catheter (TWOC), and on removal the patient is unable to void resulting in the catheter being reinserted, this **must** be coded using the following codes and sequencing:

> **M47.3   Removal of urethral catheter from bladder**
> **M47.9   Unspecified urethral catheterisation of bladder**

Examples:

Patient admitted for a right total knee replacement using cement. Two days after surgery the patient develops postoperative urinary retention that requires catheterisation. The catheter is removed prior to discharge:

> **W40.1   Primary total prosthetic replacement of knee using cement**
> **Z94.2   Right sided operation**
> **M47.9   Unspecified urethral catheterisation of bladder**
> **M47.3   Removal of urethral catheter from bladder**

Patient with enlarged prostate. Routine admission for TURP (transurethral resection of prostate). Patient catheterised (as is normal practice following the procedure). Catheter removed prior to discharge:

> **M65.3   Endoscopic resection of prostate NEC**

Routine admission for TURP (transurethral resection of prostate). Patient catheterised (as is normal practice following the procedure). Catheter removed prior to discharge, but patient fails to void. Catheter reinserted and patient is discharged with catheter in situ. To return in one week for removal.

> **M65.3   Endoscopic resection of prostate NEC**
> **M47.9   Unspecified urethral catheterisation of bladder**

Admitted for trial without urethral catheter (TWOC). Patient still unable to void and catheter is reinserted.

> **M47.3   Removal of urethral catheter from bladder**
> **M47.9   Unspecified urethral catheterisation of bladder**

PCSM7: Injection of bulking agent for stress urinary incontinence (M56.3 and M66.3)

The injection of inert soft-tissue urethral bulking agents (such as macroplastique and bioplastique) into the urethra in the treatment of stress urinary incontinence is coded as follows:

Female:

M56.3   Endoscopic injection of inert substance into outlet of female bladder

Male:

M66.3   Endoscopic injection of inert substance into outlet of male bladder

PCSM8: Transurethral incision of male bladder neck and prostate (M66.2)

Transurethral male bladder neck and prostate incision (TUIP) is coded using the following codes and sequencing:

M66.2   Endoscopic incision of outlet of male bladder NEC
Z42.2   Prostate

PCSM9: Radioactive seed implantation into prostate (M70.6)

Radioactive seed implantation into prostate is a form of interstitial brachytherapy (radiotherapy) and must be coded as follows:

M70.6   Radioactive seed implantation into prostate
        Note: Use an additional code to specify radiotherapy delivery (X65)
X65.3   Delivery of a fraction of interstitial radiotherapy
        Note: Use a subsidiary code to identify introduction of radioactive material (Y35, Y36)
Y36.3   Radioactive seed implantation NOC
Y89.-   Brachytherapy (when the dose rate is stated as being high dose or pulsed dose)

See also PCSX20: Radiotherapy (X65, X67–X68).

Radioactive seed implantation into prostate (M70.6) involves the implantation of radioactive seeds into the prostate gland which are placed via hollow needles inserted through the skin. The needles are then removed while the seeds remain in place permanently, eventually becoming biologically inert.

Implantation of radioactive substance into prostate (M71.2) involves the insertion of a thin plastic tube(s) into the prostate gland. A radioactive source is then placed into each tube. After treatment is complete the tubes are removed, leaving no radioactive material in the prostate gland.

PCSM10: Non-endoscopic microwave prostatectomy (M70.8)

Non-endoscopic microwave prostatectomy performed blind via the urethra, or transrectally is coded using the following codes and sequencing:

M70.8   Other specified other operations on outlet of male bladder
Y11.6   Microwave destruction of organ NOC.

CHAPTER N
Male Genital Organs
(N01–N35)

Coding standards and guidance

PCSN1: Injection of papaverine for impotence (N32.4)

Injection of papaverine for impotence is coded using the following code:

N32.4   Injection of therapeutic substance into penis

CHAPTER P
Lower Female Genital Tract
(P01–P32)

Chapter standards and guidance

Pessaries inserted into the vagina for antiseptic, contraceptive or abortifacient purposes are coded to Chapter Q.

Vaginal procedures carried out to support the outlet of the female bladder, for example, stress incontinence, must be classified to Chapter M.

Coding standards and guidance

PCSP1: Refashioning of episiotomy scar

Refashioning of an episiotomy scar is coded using the following codes and sequencing:

P13.8   Other specified other operations on female perineum
S60.4   Refashioning of scar NEC

PCSP2: Oversewing of exposed prosthetic mesh from previous vaginal prolapse repair (P22.8, P23.8 and P24.8)

Oversewing of exposed prosthetic mesh from previous vaginal prolapse repair must be coded using one of the following codes depending on the site of repair:

P22.8   Other specified repair of prolapse of vagina and amputation of cervix uteri
P23.8   Other specified other repair of prolapse of vagina
P24.8   Other specified repair of vault of vagina

Code **Y25.2 Resuture of organ NOC** must be assigned in addition and sequenced after one of the codes listed above.

Where pieces of prosthetic mesh have become exposed the clinician can repair this by oversewing the mesh with vaginal epithelium.

Upper Female Genital Tract
(Q01–Q56)

Coding standards and guidance

PCSQ1: Colposcopy with punch biopsy (Q03.4 and Q55.4)

Colposcopy and punch biopsy of the cervix must be coded using the following codes and sequencing:

Q03.4	**Punch biopsy of cervix uteri**
Q55.4	**Colposcopy of cervix**

PCSQ2: Dilation, curettage (D&C), hysteroscopy and intrauterine coil (Q10.3, Q10.8, Q18.8, Q18.9, Q12)

Dilation and curettage (D&C) and hysteroscopy can be coded differently depending on the reason for the procedure(s) being performed. The following codes and sequencing apply:

Diagnostic D&C only:

Q10.8	**Other specified curettage of uterus**

Therapeutic D&C only:

Q10.3	**Dilation of cervix uteri and curettage of uterus NEC**

Diagnostic D&C and diagnostic hysteroscopy:

Q18.8	**Other specified diagnostic endoscopic examination of uterus**

Therapeutic D&C and diagnostic hysteroscopy:

Q10.3	**Dilation of cervix uteri and curettage of uterus NEC**
Q18.9	**Unspecified diagnostic endoscopic examination of uterus**

Hysteroscopy only:

Q18.9	**Unspecified diagnostic endoscopic examination of uterus**

Unspecified D&C:

Q10.3	**Dilation of cervix uteri and curettage of uterus NEC**

Unspecified D&C and hysteroscopy:

Q18.9	**Unspecified diagnostic endoscopic examination of uterus**

Where an intrauterine coil procedure (insertion, replacement or removal) is performed during the same theatre visit as a diagnostic or therapeutic hysteroscopy, the hysteroscopy code must be sequenced before the intrauterine coil code.

PCSQ2: *continued*

Dilation and curettage (D&C) and hysteroscopy can be performed for diagnostic or therapeutic purposes: however, there are often occasions where this can be a combination of the two. For example, a uterine curettage can be performed to provide a tissue sample for diagnostic purposes, but it is also hoped the removal of this tissue will have some therapeutic benefits.

A hysteroscopy will always be carried out in a hospital setting by a gynaecologist. In contrast, the insertion, replacement or removal of an intrauterine contraceptive device (coil) is a relatively minor procedure which is often performed outside of a hospital setting, such as at a GP surgery or community contraceptive clinic. An intrauterine coil can have therapeutic benefits for patients with menorrhagia and dysmenorrhoea, and may be inserted during the same theatre visit as a hysteroscopy that was performed to investigate and/or treat these conditions.

PCSQ3: In vitro fertilisation (Q13.1, Q21.1 and Q38.3)

A code from category **Y96 In vitro fertilisation (IVF)** must be assigned in a subsidiary position with codes **Q13.1 Transfer of embryo to uterus NEC**, **Q21.1 Transmyometrial transfer of embryo to uterus** and **Q38.3 Endoscopic intrafallopian transfer of gametes** to classify the *type* of fertilisation involved.

PCSQ4: Magnetic Resonance Image-guided Focused Ultrasound to lesion of the uterus (Q20.6)

Magnetic resonance image-guided focused ultrasound [MRgFUS] to lesion of the uterus must be coded using the following codes and sequencing:

> **Q20.6   Focused ultrasound to lesion of uterus**
> **Y53.7   Approach to organ under magnetic resonance imaging control**

PCSQ5: Genital swab (Q55.6)

The code **Q55.6 Genital swab** must only be used for outpatient coding, or if the patient is admitted solely for the purpose of this procedure.

Gestational age (Y95)

Codes in category **Y95 Gestational age** must be assigned with various codes in Chapter Q – *see PCSY11:* **Gestational age (Y95).**

Female Genital Tract Associated with Pregnancy, Childbirth and Puerperium

(R01–R43)

Chapter standards and guidance

Emergency procedures

Separate categories exist within this chapter to classify emergency procedures. *See PGCS15: Emergency procedures*.

PChSR1: Coding deliveries (R17-R25)

All live born infants, regardless of the number of week's gestation, must be coded as a delivery.

For all delivery episodes:

- A code from categories **R17-R25** must be assigned in a primary procedural position

- Code **R24.9 All normal delivery** must only be assigned for a normal delivery, i.e. when no other code in categories **R17–R25** describing the delivery applies

- If one type of delivery method is used and subsequently changed to another type; only the method used to successfully deliver the baby must be recorded.

When coding caesarean sections:

- Assign a code from category **R17 Elective caesarean delivery** for caesarean sections performed when the patient IS NOT in labour.

- Assign a code from category **R18 Other caesarean delivery** for caesarean sections performed when the patient IS in labour (and for all emergency caesarean sections).

When coding multiple deliveries (twins, triplets):

- Each *different* type of delivery must be recorded with the *most serious* being sequenced *first*.

- Where all methods of delivery are identical, only one code is required.

The definition of a normal delivery is the process of giving birth without mechanical intervention with a vertex (top of the head) presentation.

Elective caesareans performed when the patient is in labour are likely to have similar risks to the mothers as emergency caesarean deliveries. It is important, therefore, to make the distinction between an elective caesarean performed when the patient is NOT in labour and an elective caesarean performed when the patient IS in labour.

Examples:

Failed ventouse delivery. Patient goes on to have an emergency lower caesarean section with delivery of a live female infant

> **R18.2   Lower uterine segment caesarean delivery NEC**

Patient, 22 weeks pregnant, normal delivery of live born premature baby

> **R24.9   All normal delivery**

Patient admitted at 40 weeks gestation for pre-planned caesarean section - labour not commenced

> **R17.9   Unspecified elective caesarean delivery**

Patient admitted in labour. Caesarean section planned previously

> **R18.9   Unspecified other caesarean delivery**

Patient admitted in labour. Emergency upper uterine segment caesarean section performed due to fetal distress.

> **R18.1   Upper uterine segment caesarean delivery NEC**

Spontaneous twin delivery, one normal, one breech

> **R20.1   Spontaneous breech delivery**
> **R24.9   All normal delivery**

Gestational age (Y95)

Codes in category **Y95 Gestational age** must be assigned with various codes in Chapter R – *see PCSY11: Gestational age (Y95)*.

Coding standards and guidance

PCSR1: Artificial rupture of membranes (R14.1)

Artificial rupture of membranes (ARM) must be coded to OPCS-4 code **R14.1 Forewater rupture of amniotic membranes**.

PCSR2: Intravenous augmentation when in labour (R15)

When a patient has already commenced in labour and intravenous augmentation is used to stimulate uterine contraction, a code from the OPCS-4 category **R15 Other induction of labour** is assigned.

PCSR3: Forceps delivery (R21)

If a type of forceps is named for cephalic deliveries (**R21–R24**), e.g. Neville Barnes, even though that type may be normally used for a mid forceps delivery, the coder must ascertain that this is in fact the case. The type of delivery, i.e. low, mid or high, and not the name of forceps used is the qualifying factor.

PCSR4: Face to pubes presentation (R23)

The delivery of a baby with an abnormal cephalic presentation described as 'face to pubes' (without using instrumentation) must be coded using a code in category **R23 Cephalic vaginal delivery with abnormal presentation of head at delivery without instrument**.

PCSR5: Episiotomy to facilitate delivery and subsequent repair (R27.1, R32)

Where an episiotomy (**R27.1**) is carried out to facilitate delivery, this must be sequenced in a secondary position to the delivery code.

The subsequent repair of an episiotomy is included within code **R27.1 Episiotomy to facilitate delivery** and therefore it must not be coded in addition.

The exception is where the episiotomy has extended to a perineal tear. In these cases a code from category **R32 Repair of obstetric laceration** must be assigned in addition, to classify the repair of the perineal tear.

PCSR6: Gentle cord traction for removal of retained placenta

Gentle cord traction performed to remove a retained placenta forms part of the management of 'normal' delivery and cannot be classified using OPCS-4 codes.

Gentle cord traction must not be confused with **R29.1 Manual removal of placenta from delivered uterus**, which includes insertion of a hand into the uterus and usually requires anaesthesia.

PCSR7: Obstetric scans (R36-R43)

Codes within categories **R36–R43** must be used for day cases and inpatients when the patient has been admitted solely for the purpose of a procedure/intervention.

When two or more obstetric scans classified within categories **R37.- Non-routine obstetric scan for fetal observations** and **R38.- Other non-routine obstetric scan** are performed during **one** scanning session, the following codes must be assigned

> **R37.2** Detailed structural scan
> **Y95.-** Gestational age

Procedures classified to categories **R36–R43** are always carried out using ultrasound therefore a code from category **Y53** is not required to identify the method of image control.

See also PCSU1: Diagnostic imaging procedures (U01–U21 and U35–U37).

These types of scans are usually performed in a maternity outpatient setting.

PCSR8: Anti-D injection following delivery (X30.1)

Anti-D injected prophylactically following delivery, abortion or miscarriage must be coded using code **X30.1 Injection of Rh immune globulin** in addition to the appropriate code(s) for the delivery, abortion or miscarriage. Anti-D injections must be recorded each time they are given.

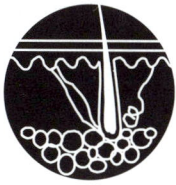

CHAPTER S
Skin
(S01–S70)

Chapter Standards and guidance

The **Note** at Chapter S states that these codes must not be used as primary codes for skin of the nipple, eyebrow and lip or for skin of the following sites, canthus, eyelid, external ear, external nose, perianal region, scrotum, male perineum, penis, vulva, female perineum, umbilicus and abdominal wall. This is because they are:

- Uniquely named and usually associated with another organ, such as the LIP which is associated with the MOUTH, and form specific categories within other chapters of the classification. For example:

  F04   Other reconstruction of lip
  Includes: Skin of lip

- Or form a major part of the (usually superficial) organ concerned, for example the EXTERNAL EAR is part of the ear, and as such is identified as a site inclusion term. For example:

  D02   Extirpation of lesion of external ear
  Includes: Skin of external ear

PChSS1: Enhancing body system codes using codes from Chapter S

When using a code from Chapter S to enhance a code from another body system chapter the code from Chapter S must be assigned:

- When it provides further information about the procedure that is not specified in the primary body system code

- In a secondary position, directly after the body system code it is enhancing.

Codes from Chapter S can be used to enhance various codes from other body system chapters. This is indicated by the note at the relevant categories in the body system chapters and at the beginning of Chapter S. For example:

  B35   Operations on nipple and areola
  Note: Codes from Chapter S may be used to enhance these codes

Examples:

Laser destruction of skin lesion of right external ear

  D02.2   Destruction of lesion of external ear
  Note: Codes from Chapter S may be used to enhance these codes
  S09.1   Laser destruction of lesion of skin of head or neck
  Z94.2   Right sided operation

Marsupialisation of skin lesion of umbilicus

  T29.3   Extirpation of lesion of umbilicus
  Includes: Skin of umbilicus
  Note: Codes from Chapter S may be used to enhance these codes
  S06.2   Marsupialisation of lesion of skin NEC

Coding standards and guidance

PCSS1: Unspecified excision of skin lesion (S06.9)

Unspecified excision of skin lesion of any site other than the head or neck must be coded as follows:

> **S06.9   Unspecified other excision of lesion of skin**
> **Z site code**
> **Z94.-   Laterality of operation** (if applicable)

Example:

Excision skin lesion of left shoulder

> **S06.9   Unspecified other excision of lesion of skin**
> **Z49.6   Skin of shoulder**
> **Z94.3   Left sided operation**

PCSS2: Phototherapy to skin (S12)

Phototherapy to skin must be coded using a code from category **S12 Phototherapy to skin**. This includes when performed for newborn jaundice.

Where the **same** type of phototherapy is administered more than once during a consultant episode, assign the relevant code from category **S12.-** once only. Where *different* types of phototherapy classified to **S12.-** are administered during the same consultant episode, assign a code for each different type of phototherapy once only.

The correct code for phototherapy treatment with a biliblanket is **S12.8 Other specified phototherapy to skin**.

PCSS3: Coding skin grafts and harvests

Skin grafts must be coded as follows:

Skin autografts (graft using material harvested from patient)

- When a specific body system skin graft code is available or when the graft is to the skin of the sites listed at the beginning of Chapter S; assign the appropriate code from the relevant **body system chapter**

- Graft code from Chapter S Skin (if doing so adds further information)*

- Chapter Z site code identifying the specific site/organ being grafted (if this has not already been identified by the body system code)

- **Z94.- Laterality of operation** (if applicable)

- Chapter Y code identifying the type of tissue harvested and the site of the harvest

- Chapter Z site code identifying the site of the harvest (if this has not already been identified within the Y harvest code)

- **Z94.- Laterality of operation** (if applicable).

PCSS3: *continued*

Other types of skin graft (skin grafts using material not harvested from patient, e.g. allograft and xenograft)

- When a specific body system skin graft code is available or when the graft is to the skin of the sites listed at the beginning of Chapter S; assign the appropriate code from the relevant **body system chapter**

- Graft code from Chapter S Skin, or (if doing so adds further information)* and/or a code from category **Y27. - Graft to organ NOC**

- Chapter Z site code identifying the specific site/organ being grafted (if this has not already been identified by the body system code)

- **Z94.- Laterality of operation** (if applicable)

An additional harvest code must not be assigned when coding skin grafts that are not autografts.

*When coding skin grafts, if a specific body system skin graft code is not available or the graft is **not** to one of the skin sites listed in the **Note** at the beginning of Chapter S, do not assign a body system chapter code; begin by assigning the graft code from Chapter S.

See also:

- *PGCS12: Coding grafts and harvests of sites other than skin*
- *PCSX12: Donation of skin (X46.2).*

Examples:

Full thickness skin graft to left canthus, graft harvested from skin of right shoulder

C11.5	Graft of skin to canthus
S36.1	Full thickness autograft of skin to head or neck
Z94.3	Left sided operation
Y58.8	Other specified harvest of skin for graft
Z49.6	Skin of shoulder
Z94.2	Right sided operation

(handwritten annotation: Body system)

Full thickness skin graft to external nose, graft harvested from right post auricular region

E09.7	Graft of skin to external nose
S36.1	Full thickness autograft of skin to head or neck
Y58.1	Harvest of full thickness skin from post auricular region
Z94.2	Right sided operation

(handwritten annotation: Body system)

Full thickness autograft to skin of back, graft harvested from right thigh

(handwritten annotation: → not body system.)

S36.2	Full thickness autograft of skin NEC
Z49.4	Skin of back
Y58.8	Other specified harvest of skin for graft
Z50.4	Skin of leg NEC
Z94.2	Right sided operation

Allograft of skin to left eyelid

C14.2	Graft of skin to eyelid
S37.1	Allograft of skin to head or neck
Z94.3	Left sided operation

Allograft of skin to back

> **S37.2** **Allograft of skin NEC**
> **Z49.4** **Skin of back**

PCSS4: Other closure of skin (S40)

Codes within this category must only be assigned to patients admitted to a paediatric ward solely for the purpose of wound closure, regardless of specialty.

PCSS5: Debridement of skin and wounds

Whenever it is stated within the patient's medical record that skin debridement has been performed, then the debridement **must** always be coded. When other procedures have taken place then the debridement must be coded in addition to these other procedures (the sequencing will depend on the main procedure performed).

Where skin graft and skin debridement have been performed, the skin graft must be selected as the primary code as this is the main procedure performed.

See also PCSS3: Coding skin grafts and harvests.

Examples:

Primary suture to laceration of scalp with removal of debris and trimming to edges of wound

> **S41.1** **Primary suture of skin of head or neck NEC**
> **Z48.1** **Skin of scalp**
> **S56.1** **Debridement of skin of head or neck NEC**
> **Z48.1** **Skin of scalp**

Primary simple repair of flexor digitorum profundus tendon and debridement of open skin wound of the right hand.

> **T67.6** **Primary simple repair of tendon**
> **Z56.4** **Flexor digitorum profundus**
> **S57.1** **Debridement of skin NEC**
> **Z50.2** **Skin of hand**
> **Z94.2** **Right sided operation**

Debridement of burnt skin of right shoulder and immediate application of split skin graft (SSG). SSG harvested from patient's right leg.

> **S35.9** **Unspecified split autograft of skin**
> **Z49.6** **Skin of shoulder**
> **Z94.2** **Right sided operation**
> **Y58.8** **Other specified harvest of skin for graft**
> **Z50.4** **Skin of leg NEC**
> **Z94.2** **Right sided operation**
> **S55.1** **Debridement of burnt skin NEC**
> **Z49.6** **Skin of shoulder**
> **Z94.2** **Right sided operation**

The following definitions apply to codes within categories **S41 Suture of skin of head or neck** and **S42 Suture of skin of other site:**

Delayed primary suture of skin

This type of suture is where wound closure is undertaken a few days after injury when risk of contamination or infection has passed, or when the wound would be under too much tension if closed immediately after injury.

Secondary suture of skin

The repair of a wound, some of which has been initially sutured, but the rest has been allowed to remain open until partially healed and covered in healthy granulations.

Resuture of skin

This is a further repair of a wound which has previously been sutured.

PCSS6: Larvae therapy of skin (S58) and Leech therapy of skin (S59)

Codes in categories **S58 Larvae therapy of skin and S59 Leech therapy of skin** must only be assigned once per hospital provider spell.

Codes **S62.7 Insertion of diagnostic device into subcutaneous tissue** and **S63.1 Removal of diagnostic device from subcutaneous tissue** include the insertion and removal of continuous blood glucose monitoring devices.

CHAPTER T
Soft Tissue
(T01–T97)

Chapter Standards and guidance

Endoscopic ultrasound staging examination

See PCSY5: Endoscopic ultrasound staging examination of organ NOC (Y41.2) for the standards for coding an endoscopic ultrasound examination (EUS) performed as a staging examination.

Coding standards and guidance

PCST1: Release of tennis elbow (T69 or W78)

If during release of tennis elbow only the tendon is released/freed this must be coded to category **T69 Freeing of tendon**. If the joint is released, this must be coded to category **W78 Release of contracture of joint**.

PCST2: Release of trigger finger (T72.3)

Release of trigger finger must be coded using **T72.3 Release of constriction of sheath of tendon**.

The term 'block dissection' does not apply to a specific number of lymph nodes. If the clinician states that they performed a block dissection it is correct to assign a code from category **T85 Block dissection of lymph nodes**, irrespective of the number of nodes removed.

PCST3: Sampling, excision, biopsy or drainage of sentinel lymph node (T86-T88, T91.1 and O14.2)

When sampling, excision, biopsy or drainage of sentinel lymph node is performed the following codes must be assigned:

> **T86-T88**
> **O14.2** Sentinel lymph node
> **Z94.-** Laterality of operation (if applicable)

T91.1 Biopsy of sentinel lymph node NEC must only be used when the exact site of the sentinel lymph node is unknown.

Example:

Excision of right sided sentinel axillary lymph node

> **T87.3** **Excision or biopsy of axillary lymph node**
> > *Note: Use subsidiary code for sentinel lymph node (O14.2)*
> **O14.2** **Sentinel lymph node**
> **Z94.2** **Right sided operation**

Scanning of sentinel lymph node (T91.2)

T91.2 Scanning of sentinel lymph node is a nuclear medicine imaging procedure and a code from categories **Y93**, **Y94**, **Y97** and **Y98** must not be assigned in addition.

See PCSU3: Nuclear medicine imaging procedures.

CHAPTER U
Diagnostic Imaging, Testing and Rehabilitation
(U01–U54)

Coding standards and guidance

PCSU1: Diagnostic imaging procedures (U01–U21 and U34–U37)

Coding diagnostic imaging procedures using body system chapter codes

When a specific code classifying a diagnostic imaging procedure is available in a body system chapter (Chapters A–T and V–W), for example **Q55.5 Transvaginal ultrasound examination of female genital tract, C87.1 Digital imaging of retina** and scanning codes within the range **R36–R43**, the body system chapter code **must** be used in preference to the codes within categories **U01–U21** and **U34–U37**.

The standard to only code diagnostic imaging procedures in an outpatient setting or if the patient has been admitted solely for the purpose of a procedure/intervention only applies to codes in categories **U01–U21** and **U34–U37** and categories **R36–R43**.

Additional codes from categories **Y97 Radiology with contrast** and **Y98 Radiology procedures** must not be assigned with body system chapter imaging codes.

See also PCSR7: Obstetric scans (R36-R43).

Coding diagnostic imaging using codes from Chapter U

Codes in the range **U01–U21** and their extended categories **U34–U37** are only for use in an outpatient setting, or if a patient has been admitted solely for the purpose of a diagnostic imaging procedure/intervention. The exceptions to this standard are:

- **Magnetic Resonance Imaging (MRI)**
- **Computed Tomography (CT)**
- **U19.1 Implantation of electrocardiography loop recorder**
- **U19.7 Removal of electrocardiography loop recorder**
- **U20.1 Transthoracic echocardiography (TTE)**
- **U20.2 Transoesophageal echocardiography (TOE)**
- **U20.3 Intravascular echocardiography**
- **U20.4 Epicardial echocardiography**

These exceptions must always be coded on inpatient and outpatient episodes of care.

The '*Notes*' at categories **U01–U21** and **U34–U37** indicate when additional codes from category **Y98 Radiology procedures** and **Y97 Radiology with contrast** (if used) are required – *see PCSU2 Radiological contrast and body areas (Y97-Y98).*

The codes in categories **U01–U21** and **U34–U37** that classify nuclear medicine imaging procedures do not require the addition of codes from categories **Y97** or **Y98** – *see PCSU3 Nuclear medicine imaging procedures.*

PCSU1: *continued*

Diagnostic imaging of one body area using one method of imaging

When **one** body site alone is scanned and this can be indexed to a code range from **U01–U18**, **U35** or **U37** assign the following codes:

- Specific body system code from **U01–U18**, **U35** or **U37**
- **Y97 Radiology with contrast** (if used)
- **Y98.1 Radiology of one body area (or < 20 minutes)**
- Z site code (if doing so adds further information).
- **Z94.- Laterality of operation** (if applicable)

An indexable body system code must only be recorded **once** for each **visit** to the scanner documented in the patient's medical record.

Diagnostic imaging of one body area using multiple different types of imaging and diagnostic imaging of multiple body areas

When one body area is scanned during a single visit to the radiology department using multiple types of imaging **or** when more than one area is scanned during a single visit to the radiology department using either the *same* or *different* types of imaging assign the following codes and sequencing for each different type of imaging used:

- The specific fourth character at **U21 Diagnostic imaging procedures** or **U36 Other diagnostic imaging procedures**
- **Y97 Radiology with contrast** (if used)
- **Y98 Radiology procedures** (with the fourth-character selection being reliant upon the number of areas scanned or duration of the scan)
- Z site code(s)
- **Z94.- Laterality of operation** (if applicable)

Specified diagnostic imaging procedures not classifiable to body site or system categories

Where a specific type of imaging is not classifiable at fourth-character level within categories **U01–U18**, **U35** or **U37**, but is available within categories **U21 Diagnostic imaging procedure** or **U36 Other diagnostic imaging procedure** assign the following codes and sequencing:

- The specific fourth character at **U21 Diagnostic imaging procedures** or **U36 Other diagnostic imaging procedures** (excluding **U21.8**)
- **Y97 Radiology with contrast** (if used).
- **Y98 Radiology procedures** (with the fourth-character selection being reliant upon the number of areas scanned)
- Z site code(s)
- **Z94.- Laterality of operation** (if applicable)

PCSU1: *continued*

Where a specific type of imaging cannot be classified at fourth-character level within categories **U01–U18**, **U35** or **U37**, and there is no fourth-character code available in category **U21** or **U36** assign the following codes and sequencing:

- Residual subcategory **.8** from categories **U01–U18**

- **Y97 Radiology with contrast** (if used).

- **Y98 Radiology procedures** (with the specific fourth-character selected being reliant upon the number of areas scanned).

Code **U21.8 Other specified diagnostic imaging procedures** must not be assigned in these circumstances.

Examples:

Computed tomography (CT) of head with pre and post contrast

U05.1	Computed tomography of head
	Note: Use subsidiary codes to identify radiology with contrast (Y97), radiology procedures (Y98)
Y97.1	Radiology with pre and post contrast
Y98.1	Radiology of one body area (or < 20 minutes)

Ultrasound elastography of the liver

U36.4	Ultrasound elastography
	Note: Use subsidiary codes to identify radiology with contrast (Y97), radiology procedures (Y98)
Y98.1	Radiology of one body area (or < 20 minutes)
Z30.1	Liver

MRI and CT of head post contrast

U21.1	Magnetic resonance imaging NEC
	Note: Use subsidiary codes to identify radiology with contrast (Y97), radiology procedures (Y98)
Y97.3	Radiology with post-contrast
Y98.1	Radiology of one body area (or < 20 minutes)
Z92.1	Head NEC
U21.2	Computed tomography NEC
	Note: Use subsidiary codes to identify radiology with contrast (Y97), radiology procedures (Y98)
Y97.3	Radiology with post-contrast
Y98.1	Radiology of one body area (or < 20 minutes)
Z92.1	Head NEC

Diagnostic ultrasound of kidneys and bladder lasting 15 minutes (Outpatient setting)

U21.6	Ultrasound scan NEC
	Note: Use subsidiary codes to identify radiology with contrast (Y97), radiology procedures (Y98)
Y98.1	Radiology of one body area (or < 20 minutes)
Z41.1	Kidney

Z94.1   **Bilateral operation**
Z42.1   **Bladder NEC**

Code **Y98.1** has been selected because the scan lasted less than 20 minutes and it is the time duration which defines which code from category **Y98.-** when coding ultrasound scans.

Diagnostic ultrasound of kidneys lasting 10 minutes with magnetic resonance imaging (MRI) of abdomen (Outpatient setting)

U21.6   **Ultrasound scan NEC**
         Note: Use subsidiary codes to identify radiology with contrast (Y97), radiology procedures (Y98)
Y98.1   **Radiology of one body area (or < 20 minutes)**
Z41.1   **Kidney**
Z94.1   **Bilateral operation**
U21.1   **Magnetic resonance imaging NEC**
         Note: Use subsidiary codes to identify radiology with contrast (Y97), radiology procedures (Y98)
Y98.1   **Radiology of one body area (or < 20 minutes)**
Z92.6   **Abdomen NEC**

Post contrast MRI of lumbar and sacral spine

U21.1   **Magnetic resonance imaging NEC**
         Note: Use subsidiary codes to identify radiology with contrast (Y97), radiology procedures (Y98)
Y97.3   **Radiology with post-contrast**
Y98.2   **Radiology of two body areas**
Z66.5   **Lumbar vertebra**
Z66.8   **Specified vertebra NEC**

Computed tomography of left deep femoral artery

U21.2   **Computed tomography NEC**
         Note: Use subsidiary codes to identify radiology with contrast (Y97), radiology procedures (Y98)
Y98.1   **Radiology of one body area (or < 20 minutes)**
Z38.4   **Deep femoral artery**
Z94.3   **Left sided operation**

PCSU2: Radiological contrast and body areas (Y97–Y98)

The '*Notes*' at categories **U01–U21** and **U34–U37** indicate when additional codes from category **Y98 Radiology procedures** and **Y97 Radiology with contrast**, if used, are required.

The codes in categories **U01–U21** and **U34–U37** that classify nuclear medicine imaging procedures do not require codes from categories **Y97** or **Y98** – *see PCSU3: Nuclear medicine imaging procedures.*

Codes from **Y97 Radiology with contrast** must always be assigned *after* the codes for the specific scan and *before* codes from *Y98 Radiology procedures.*

OPCS-4 codes from categories **Y97 Radiology with contrast** and **Y98 Radiology procedures** must not be used with the diagnostic imaging codes from the body system Chapters A–T and V–W.

PCSU2: *continued*

Y97 Radiology with contrast:

Codes within category **Y97** must only be assigned if it is stated in the patient's medical record that the imaging procedure has been performed using contrast media. Codes in category **Y97** must be used as follows:

- **Y97.1 Radiology with pre and post contrast** is assigned when image(s) are taken before contrast is given and then again after contrast has been introduced.

- **Y97.3 Radiology with post contrast** is assigned when image(s) are taken after contrast is given.

- When only 'radiology with contrast' is stated in the medical record **Y97.3 Radiology with post contrast** must be used as the default.

The following codes from category **Y97** <u>must</u> not be used:

- **Y97.2 Radiology with pre contrast** as this classifies image(s) taken before contrast is given.

- **Y97.8 Other specified radiology with contrast** and **Y97.9 Unspecified radiology with contrast** as the type of contrast would be coded using **Y97.1** or **Y97.3**.

Y98 Radiology procedures:

Codes within **Y98** are used to classify the following:

- number of body areas scanned/examined or the duration of the scan

- mobile and intraoperative scans

- extensive patient repositioning.

Codes **Y98.1**, **Y98.3** and **Y98.5** are used interchangeably to identify the time duration of the scan or the number of body areas examined during the scan.

When coding ultrasound and contrast fluoroscopy, it is the time duration and not the number of body areas that defines which code from category **Y98** must be assigned.

In the case of magnetic resonance imaging, computed tomography and plain x-ray, it is the number of body areas scanned that defines which code must be assigned, irrespective of the time duration taken to perform these scans.

The 'body areas' referred to in the codes in category **Y98** relate to the following nine anatomical regions of the body. These must be used as a guide during code assignment:

- **Head**

- **Neck (including cervical spine)**

- **Thorax (including thoracic spine)**

- **Abdomen (including lumbar spine)**

- **Pelvic region (including all organs in genitourinary system, sacral spine and groin)**

- **Right leg**

- **Left leg**

- **Right arm**

- **Left arm.**

PCSU2: *continued*

It is important the default code **Y98.1 Radiology of one body area (or < 20 minutes)** is selected if the area /duration of scan is not specified. It is the responsibility of the clinician to provide this level of detail in the source document.

Where different methods of radiological imaging are carried out, each method must have a code from **Y98 Radiology procedures** assigned.

Y98.6 Mobile and or intraoperative procedures of any/all body areas and **Y98.7 Extensive patient repositioning to obtain required image series** are used as additional codes to any other codes in category **Y98** when this information has been provided in the medical record. It is therefore permissible for more than one code to be assigned from category **Y98 Radiology procedures** on the same episode of care.

It is important to be very precise about radiology procedures, as a common term like 'x-ray' can apply to diverse procedures such as: plain film x-ray, contrast media x-ray, fluoroscopic x-ray, mammography x-ray or CT scan x-ray.

Care must be taken when assigning codes for procedures which are performed using a fluoroscopic approach and contrast fluoroscopy scans, as the latter is simply a diagnostic image of a body area.

Examples:

Computed tomography (CT) of head

> **U05.1** **Computed tomography of head**
> > *Note: Use subsidiary codes to identify radiology with contrast (Y97), radiology procedures (Y98)*
> **Y98.1** **Radiology of one body area (or < 20 minutes)**

Magnetic resonance imaging (MRI) of chest with extensive patient repositioning (pre and post contrast)

> **U07.2** **Magnetic resonance imaging of chest**
> > *Note: Use subsidiary codes to identify radiology with contrast (Y97), radiology procedures (Y98)*
> **Y97.1** **Radiology with pre and post contrast**
> **Y98.1** **Radiology of one body area (or < 20 minutes)**
> **Y98.7** **Extensive patient repositioning to obtain required image series**

Contrast fluoroscopy scan of the oesophagus lasting 35 minutes

> **U21.5** **Contrast fluoroscopy NEC**
> > *Note: Use subsidiary codes to identify radiology with contrast (Y97), radiology procedures (Y98)*
> **Y98.3** **Radiology of three body areas (or 20-40 minutes)**
> **Z27.1** **Oesophagus**

PCSU3: Nuclear medicine imaging procedures (U01–U21 and U34–U37)

Nuclear medicine imaging codes in the range **U01–U21** and their extended categories **U34–U37** are only for use in an outpatient setting, or if a patient has been admitted solely for the purpose of a nuclear medicine imaging procedure. The exceptions to this standard are:

- **Positron Emission Tomography (PET)**

- **Single photon emission computed tomography (SPECT)**

- **Positron emission tomography with computed tomography (PET/CT)**

- **Single photon emission computed tomography with computed tomography (SPECT/CT)**

These exceptions must always be coded on inpatient and outpatient episodes of care.

Codes that classify nuclear medicine procedures within categories **U01–U21** and **U34–U37** are identified by the presence of the '**Note**' indicating to use a subsidiary code to identify **Y93 Gallium-67 imaging** or **Y94 Radiopharmaceutical imaging**. These subsidiary codes must be used if radiopharmaceutical imaging substances are used during a nuclear medicine imaging procedure.

Codes from categories **Y97 Radiology with contrast** or **Y98 Radiology procedures** must not be assigned in addition to nuclear medicine codes, *see PCSU1 Diagnostic imaging procedures (U01–U21 and U34–U37) and PCSU2: Radiological contrast and body areas (Y97–Y98).*

See also PCSU4: Myocardial/Cardiac perfusion scan (U10.6 and U11.5).

Nuclear medicine imaging procedures available in the main body system chapters are **B16.4 Parathyroid washout** and **T91.2 Scanning of sentinel lymph node**. Codes from categories **Y93**, **Y94**, **Y97** and **Y98** must not be assigned in addition to the nuclear medicine imaging codes contained within the body system chapters.

Example:

Thyroid nuclear scan using octreotide imaging.

> **U06.5**   **Scanning of thyroid gland NEC**
> > *Note: Use subsidiary codes to identify gallium-67 imaging (Y93), radiopharmaceutical imaging (Y94)*
> **Y94.2**   **Octreotide imaging**

PCSU4: Myocardial/Cardiac perfusion scan (U10.6 and U11.5)

If only the first phase (the stress test) of the perfusion scan is carried out, this must be coded to **U11.5 Thallium stress test**.

If both phases are carried out (the stress test and rest tests) code **U10.6 Myocardial perfusion scan** must be assigned instead, irrespective of the agent used. Where a different agent to thallium is used a code from categories **Y93 Gallium-67 imaging** or **Y94 Radiopharmaceutical imaging** must be assigned in addition.

Codes **U10.6** and **U11.5** are only for use in an outpatient setting, or if a patient has been admitted solely for the purpose of the test/scan. *See also PCSU3: Nuclear medicine imaging procedures.*

Myocardial/Cardiac perfusion scans are carried out in two phases: a stress test and a rest test. As well as the radiopharmaceutical Thallium, MIBI and Tetrofosmin are also commonly used for stress tests and are commonly referred to as myocardial perfusion agents.

PCSU5: Diagnostic tests (U22-U33 and U40)

Codes in categories **U22–U33** and **U40** classify diagnostic tests and are only for use in an outpatient setting, or for day cases and inpatients if a patient has been admitted solely for the purpose of the diagnostic test.

The exception is code **U22.1 Electroencephalograph telemetry** which must always be coded on inpatient and outpatient hospital episodes.

EEG telemetry (**U22.1**) is a specialised investigation provided by neurophysiology centres. It is used in the diagnosis of epilepsy, for assessing patients for possible surgical treatments for epilepsy and also for the diagnosis of neurological disorders of sleep. The patient is admitted to hospital where EEG and simultaneous video telemetry is recorded continuously for the entire length of stay. This is usually 3–5 days but can be for a period of up to 21 days. *See also Chapter A for guidance on Electroencephalography NEC (A84.1).*

PCSU6: Diagnostic blood tests (U32.1, X36.3, X36.8 and X36.9)

Diagnostic blood tests must **only** be coded when the patient is **admitted solely for the purpose of** the diagnostic blood test, using the following OPCS-4 codes:

U32.1	**Human Immunodeficiency Virus blood test**
X36.3	**Venous sampling**
X36.8	**Other specified blood withdrawal**
X36.9	**Unspecified blood withdrawal**

Codes **U32.1 Human Immunodeficiency Virus blood test** and **X36.3 Venous sampling**, must only be assigned when these tests are explicitly documented in the patient's medical record or when the responsible consultant has confirmed that these tests have been performed.

Code **X36.8 Other specified blood withdrawal** is assigned when another specified type of blood test, which is not a Human Immunodeficiency Virus blood test or Venous sampling, has been performed.

If the type of diagnostic blood test is not specified, then OPCS-4 code **X36.9 Unspecified blood withdrawal** must be assigned.

Sleep disorders involving respiratory functions, such as sleep apnoea, are normally conducted by a specialist Respiratory team using polysomnography or cardiopulmonary sleep studies which are classified at code **U33.1 Polysomnography**. The emphasis of this test will be towards diagnosing sleep disordered breathing. *See also Chapter A for guidance on Sleep studies (A84.7).*

PCSU7: Rehabilitation (U50–U54)

Rehabilitation codes **U50–U54** must *only* be used when a patient is either:

- admitted to a rehabilitation unit solely for the purpose of rehabilitation

  or

- is transferred to a rehabilitation specialty either within the same trust or at a different trust.

They must be assigned on each consultant episode in which the patient is undergoing rehabilitation.

Where a patient receives rehabilitation assessment (**X60**) and rehabilitation delivery (**U50–U54**) within the same admission, only one code is required, with that code being from **U50–U54**, as it is assumed the assessment would have been carried out before the rehabilitation commenced. *See also PCSX18: Rehabilitation Assessment (X60).*

Examples:

Emergency admission for intracapsular fracture neck of femur, treated with closed reduction and fixation using dynamic hip screw. Rehabilitation using physiotherapy during same episode.

W24.1   Closed reduction of intracapsular fracture of neck of femur and fixation using nail or screw

Drug addict admitted to rehabilitation unit for assessment. Rehabilitation programme written and patient starts treatment immediately.

U52.1   Delivery of rehabilitation for drug addiction

Patient is admitted solely for the purpose of rehabilitation following a total hip replacement for osteoarthritis of the hip

U50.3   Delivery of rehabilitation for joint replacement

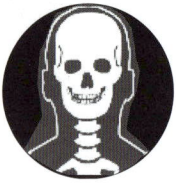

CHAPTER V
Bones and Joints of Skull and Spine
(V01–V68)

Chapter standards and guidance

PChSV1: Levels of spine (V55)

Whenever a code from categories **V22–V68** is assigned a code from category **V55 Levels of spine** must be assigned directly afterwards to indicate the number of levels operated on.

When the level of spine is not specified, code **V55.9 Unspecified levels of spine** must be assigned.

It is strongly recommended that coding managers work closely with the relevant orthopaedic surgeons to ensure that this information is clearly documented in the source document to allow accurate assignment of the correct fourth character.

A 'level of spine' means either a **vertebra**, a **disc**, or a **motion segment**

Operations carried out on **vertebrae** include:

- Vertebral excision

- Decompression of fractured vertebrae

- Reduction and fixation of fractured vertebrae

- Biopsy of vertebrae.

Laminectomy or laminectomy decompression (not 'laminectomy approach') usually does not involve a procedure on the disc, the decompression is the removal of the bone (lamina) and flavum at the back of the spinal canal, however the decompression occurs at disc level. Therefore, a laminectomy decompression is related to a disc level.

Operations carried out on **intervertebral discs** include:

- Disc excision

- Disc replacement

- Foraminoplasty

- Coblation to disc

- Discography.

Operations carried out on **motion segments** (an intervertebral joint consisting of two vertebrae and the intervening disc) include:

- Decompression of vertebra-disc-vertebra sections

- Interspinous process spacer insertions

- Facet joint injections.

Examples:

Kyphoplasty of fracture of vertebra of thoracic spine

V44.5	**Balloon kyphoplasty of fracture of spine**
V55.9	**Unspecified levels of spine**
Z66.4	**Thoracic vertebra**

Kyphoplasty of fractures of second, fifth and tenth vertebrae of thoracic spine (T2, T5 and T10)

V44.5	**Balloon kyphoplasty of fracture of spine**
V55.3	**Greater than two levels of spine**
Z66.4	**Thoracic vertebra**

Primary posterior laminectomy decompression of L4/L5 spine

V25.4	**Primary posterior laminectomy decompression of lumbar spine**
V55.1	**One level of spine**

Automated percutaneous mechanical excision of L4/L5 lumbar intervertebral disc under image control

V58.3	**Primary automated percutaneous mechanical excision of lumbar intervertebral disc**
V55.1	**One level of spine**
Y53.9	**Unspecified approach to organ under image control**

Microdiscectomy of L1/L2 and L4/L5 lumbar intervertebral discs and C6/C7 cervical intervertebral disc

V33.7	**Primary microdiscectomy of lumbar intervertebral disc**
V55.2	**Two levels of spine**
V29.6	**Primary microdiscectomy of cervical intervertebral disc**
V55.1	**One level of spine**

Insertion of L1/2 interspinous process spacer

V28.1	**Primary insertion of lumbar interspinous process spacer**
V55.1	**One level of spine**

Posterior instrumented fusion of lumbar L4/5 and thoracic T1/2 and T2/3 motion segment

V40.4	**Posterior instrumented fusion of lumbar spine NEC**
V55.1	**One level of spine**
V40.3	**Posterior instrumented fusion of thoracic spine NEC**
V55.2	**Two levels of spine**

PChSV2: Discectomy for decompression

When discectomy is performed in order to decompress, only the code that classifies the spinal decompression operation is necessary, as long as the following criteria are met:

- The decompression and discectomy must have been performed on the *same* disc or group of vertebrae or motion segment

and

- The responsible consultant must have stated that discectomy was performed in order to result in decompression.

Generally speaking, decompression is "removal of pressure" and removal of the disc is a form of decompression. For example, if the cervical spinal cord or cervical spinal nerve roots are compressed anteriorly by a disc or osteophyte, then the most common operation is anterior cervical discectomy (or corpectomy) as an anterior approach to decompress the cord/root.

PChSV3: Instrumented spinal fusions with decompression and bone graft

When a spinal decompression is performed in addition to a spinal fusion and instrumentation procedure, it is **only** necessary to assign an additional code for the spinal decompression if the code description (for the fusion/instrumentation procedure) does not state **both** 'fusion' **and** 'decompression'.

A bone graft (synthetic or allograft) is an integral part of the spinal fusion and instrumentation procedure. Therefore it is **not** necessary to assign an additional OPCS-4 code for the bone graft when it is performed together with spinal fusion and instrumentation. However, in instances where an **autograft** has been used during the fusion and instrumentation procedure, it is necessary to assign an additional OPCS-4 code from category **Y66 Harvest of bone** to identify the location where the bone was harvested from.

Examples:

Patient admitted for L5/S1 Transforaminal Lumbar Interbody Fusion (TLIF) with posterior decompression of lumbar spine.

V38.6	**Primary transforaminal interbody fusion of joint of lumbar spine**
V55.1	**One level of spine**
V25.5	**Primary posterior decompression of lumbar spine NEC**
V55.1	**One level of spine**

Posterior lumbar spinal decompression with intertransverse fusion

V25.3	**Primary posterior decompression of lumbar spine and intertransverse fusion of joint of lumbar spine.**
V55.9	**Unspecified levels of spine**

Patient admitted for L3/L5 primary anterior lumbar interbody fusion (ALIF) and posterior instrumentation with the use of bone autograft from the right iliac crest

V33.6	**Primary anterior excision of lumbar intervertebral disc and posterior instrumentation of lumbar spine**
V55.2	**Two levels of spine**
Y66.3	**Harvest of bone from iliac crest**
Z94.2	**Right sided operation**

Image control used for checking position of reduced fractures and the correct siting of fixators

See:

- *PCSY7: Approach to organ under image control (Y53 and Y78).*

Coding standards and guidance

There are a number of different techniques used for remodelling of the skull including barrel staving, pi-extension, melon-slicing, rotation, swapping, re-contouring, re-situating and plication. It is not necessary to assign additional codes to identify the specific type of remodelling used.

V02.1 Posterior calvarial release is usually performed as the first stage of a staged procedure and a more substantial remodelling procedure will be performed at a later date. *See PGCS18: Staged procedures.*

Example:

First stage posterior calvarial release for craniosynostosis, with application of external distractors.

> **V02.1**   **Posterior calvarial release**
> **V18.1**   **Application of external distracters to skull**
> **Y70.3**   **First stage of staged operations NOC**

PCSV1: Temporal bone excision (V05.8)

Temporal bone excision must be coded using the following codes and sequencing:

> **V05.8**   **Other specified other operations on cranium**
> **Y05.-**   **Excision of organ NOC**
> **Z63.3**   **Temporal bone**
> **Z94.-**   **Laterality of operation**

PCSV2: LeFort osteotomies (V10.2, V10.3 and V10.4)

The following codes classify LeFort osteotomies:

- **LeFort I**   –   **V10.4 Low level osteotomy of maxilla**

- **Lefort II**   –   **V10.3 Osteotomy of maxilla involving nasal complex**

- **LeFort III**   –   **V10.2 Transorbital subcranial osteotomy of bone of face**

As with all eponyms the coder must ensure that code assignment fully reflects the procedure performed. ***See PRule 8: Surgical eponyms.***

Example:

LeFort I low level osteotomy of maxilla with application of intermaxillary fixation.

> **V10.4**   **Low level osteotomy of maxilla**
> **V11.1**   **Intermaxillary fixation of maxilla**

PCSV3: Repair of craniofacial cleft and reconstruction of cranial and facial bones (V12.3 and V12.4)

When a transcranial and subcranial repair of craniofacial cleft and reconstruction of cranial and facial bones have been performed codes **V12.3 Transcranial repair of craniofacial cleft and reconstruction of cranial and facial bones HFQ** and **V12.4 Subcranial repair of craniofacial cleft and reconstruction of cranial and facial bones HFQ** must both be assigned.

Where excision/resection of encephalocele is performed at the same time as transcranial and/or subcranial repair of craniofacial cleft and reconstruction of cranial and facial bones a code from category **A06 Other excision of lesion of tissue of brain** must be assigned before codes **V12.3** or **V12.4**.

There is no sequencing standard when assigning codes **V12.3** and **V12.4** together, sequencing will usually be based on what was documented first in the patient's medical record.

Code **V17.1 Intermaxillary fixation of mandible** includes the use of eyelet or tie wires. **V17.2 Internal fixation of mandible NEC** includes the use of Champey plates, screws and plates. **V17.3 Extraoral fixation of mandible** includes outside splints, such as halo.

PCSV4: Primary percutaneous endoscopic excision of thoracic intervertebral disc using laser (V31.4)

When **V31.4 Primary percutaneous endoscopic excision of thoracic intervertebral disc** is performed using a laser **Y08.1 Laser excision of organ NOC** must be assigned in addition.

PCSV5: Lumbar interbody fusion (V33.3, V33.6, V38.5, V38.6 and V51.1)

V33.3 Primary anterior excision of lumbar intervertebral disc and interbody fusion of joint of lumbar spine classifies:

- Anterior lumbar interbody fusion (ALIF)

- Stand alone anterior lumbar interbody fusion (STALIF)

- Axial lumbar interbody fusion (AXIALIF). Additional codes for instrumentation must **not** be assigned.

V33.6 Primary anterior excision of lumbar intervertebral disc and posterior instrumentation of lumbar spine classifies:

- Anterior lumbar interbody fusion (ALIF) with posterior instrumentation.

V38.5 Primary posterior interbody fusion of joint of lumbar spine classifies:

- Posterior lumbar interbody fusion (PLIF).

V38.6 Primary transforaminal interbody fusion of joint of lumbar spine classifies:

- Transforaminal lumbar interbody fusion (TLIF).

V51.1 Primary direct lateral excision of lumbar intervertebral disc and interbody fusion of joint of lumbar spine classifies:

- Direct lumbar interbody fusion (DLIF)

Additional codes for instrumentation must **not** be assigned when coding these procedures.

When assigning codes from category **V40 Stabilisation of spine** if the instrumented fusion is not stated to be 'posterior' it should be **assumed** to be posterior. Posterior instrumented fusion can also be seen documented as postero-lateral instrumented fusion or intertransverse instrumented fusion.

Codes in category **V41 Instrumental correction of deformity of spine** classify instrumented correction of spinal deformities, such as kyphosis and scoliosis, and must not be used to classify instrumented spinal fusions which can be found at category **V40 Stabilisation of spine**.

Code **V41.1 Posterior attachment of correctional instrument to spine** includes 'Harrington rod' and 'Hartshill triangle'.

PCSV6: Magnetic adjustment of spinal growing system (V41.6)

Magnetic adjustment of spinal growing system must be coded using the following codes:

V41.6	**Attention to spinal growing system**
V55.-	**Levels of spine**
Y03.6	**Adjustment to prosthesis in organ NOC**

Codes **V41.5 Posterior attachment of spinal growing system**, **V41.6 Attention to spinal growing system** and **V41.7 Surgical distraction of spinal growing system** classify growing/lengthening rods; these are magnetically or surgically adjustable systems that are inserted posteriorly into the spine of younger patients for the treatment of scoliosis. Following insertion these can be elongated at specific intervals by the clinician using either surgical distraction in theatre or more commonly using magnets in an outpatient clinic.

Pain relief procedures

For the standard for the coding of facet joint block *see PCSA2: Pain relief procedures*.

CHAPTER W
Other Bones and Joints
(W01–W99, O06–O10, O17–O19, O21–O27, O29, O32)

Chapter standards and guidance

PChSW1: K-wire fixation

K-wire fixation must always be coded as **rigid fixation**. When K-wires are used to augment anchorage of cerclage wires or in skeletal traction, the use of K-wires must not be coded in addition.

Example:

Primary closed reduction and K-wire fixation of right sided fracture of lower end of radius, performed under image intensifier

W24.2	**Closed reduction of fracture of long bone and rigid internal fixation NEC**
Y53.5	**Approach to organ under image intensifier**
Z70.5	**Lower end of radius NEC**
Z94.2	**Right sided operation**

PChSW2: Arthroscopic procedures (W84.8)

For procedures performed arthroscopically, code **W84.8 Other specified therapeutic endoscopic operations on other joint structure** must only be assigned when:

- There is no specific 4th character endoscopic (arthroscopic) code that classifies the procedure

- There is no specific 4th character open code that classifies the procedure

- There is no **.8 Other specified** code in any other endoscopic or open category that describes the organ or structure on which the procedure is performed

See PGCS1: Endoscopic and minimal access operations that do not have a specific code.

Example:

Endoscopic replacement of right meniscus using allograft from cadaver

W82.8	**Other specified therapeutic endoscopic operations on semilunar cartilage**
Y01.6	**Alloreplacement of organ from cadaver NOC**
Z94.2	**Right sided operation**
W82.8	has been assigned as it provides a greater level of specificity about the organ/structure operated on (semilunar cartilage) than **W84.8 Other specified therapeutic endoscopic operations on other joint structure.**

PChSW3: Procedures using multiple types of fixation

If during a fixation procedure more than one type/ component of a fixation device has been used (e.g. pin and plate, pins and 'K' wires) only the main part of the device that is holding the fracture together must be coded.

When it is not clear which part of the fixation device is the main part holding the fracture together, advice must be sought from the responsible consultant.

For example, in a fractured femur that is pinned and plated it is the pin that is coded. In an Ilizarov fixator, it is the external part of the device that is holding the fracture, and therefore this is coded as an external fixator.

Types of bone reduction and fixation in the treatment of fractures:

Reduction:

- *Closed* reduction consists of manual manipulation of the fracture and is usually performed in an operating theatre with the use of anaesthesia.

- *Open* reduction includes an open surgical operation for reducing and immobilising the fracture. Complete fracture immobilisation is commonly carried out by combining reduction procedures with various methods of fixation.

Fixation: Biocompatible fixators may be used externally or internally to hold fragments of bone in position until union takes place.

- *Internal* fixation includes inserting screws, plates, pins, wires and nails into the bone to hold the fracture in place. *Intramedullary* and *extramedullary* fixation are both forms of internal fixation.

- *External* fixation involves a fixation device outside of the bone. It includes braces, plates, and fixators such as Ilizarov.

Both external and internal fixation may be performed with either open or closed procedures for fractures.

Image control used for checking position of reduced fractures and the correct siting of fixators

See PCSY7: Approach to organ under image control (Y53 and Y78)

Conversion procedures

See PGCS16: Conversion procedures for standards for coding conversion procedures.

Coding procedures performed for the correction of congenital deformities

See PGCS11: Coding procedures performed for the correction of congenital deformities.

Coding standards and guidance

PCSW12: Osteotomy of the foot

When coding foot osteotomies, the appropriate OPCS-4 category will depend on the method of osteotomy and whether the osteotomy was performed on a single metatarsal, on multiple metatarsals, or on the phalanges.

There are many codes within Chapters W and X that specifically describe different methods of osteotomy, e.g. angulation periarticular osteotomy (**W12.-**) or displacement osteotomy (**W13.2**); these terms must be documented in the patient's medical record and the appropriate index trail must be followed to assign these codes.

Osteotomies are often documented with the use of eponyms: however, the use of eponyms (e.g. Akin osteotomy, Scarf osteotomy) within clinical coding is discouraged. Where an eponym has been used by the responsible consultant and the specific type of osteotomy (e.g.'displacement', 'periarticular angulation' etc) has also been stated, rather than using the Alphabetical Index of Surgical Eponyms, the clinical coder must assign codes for the specific type of osteotomy using the Alphabetical Index of Interventions and Procedures.

See also PRule 8: Surgical eponyms

Osteotomies of the foot must be coded as follows:

Osteotomy/ osteotomies of multiple metatarsals of the same foot

All osteotomy/ osteotomies carried out on more than one metatarsal of the same foot must be assigned the following codes, regardless of the method used:

> **W03.2 Osteotomy of multiple metatarsals** or **W03.6 Osteotomy of multiple metatarsals and fixation HFQ**
> Z site code (where this adds further information)
> **Z94.-   Laterality of operation**

Osteotomy/ osteotomies of a single metatarsal, specified method

For osteotomy/ osteotomies of a single metatarsal, where the method of osteotomy is specified the following codes must be assigned. The OPCS-4 Alphabetical Index must be used to assign the appropriate osteotomy code:

> **W12.-   Angulation periarticular division of bone** or **W13.- Other periarticular division of bone** or **W14.- Diaphyseal division of bone** or **W77.5 Periarticular osteotomy for stabilisation of joint**
> Z site code (where this adds further information)
> **W28.1 Application of internal fixation to bone NEC** or **W30.1 Application of external fixation to bone NEC** (if fixation is used, and is not already implicit in the osteotomy code description)
> Z site code (where this adds further information)
> **Z94.-   Laterality of operation**

PCSW12: *continued*

Osteotomy/ osteotomies of a single metatarsal, unspecified method

Osteotomy/ osteotomies of a single metatarsal, where the method of the osteotomy/ osteotomies is not specified, must be coded as follows:

W15.-   Division of bone of foot*
Z site code (where this adds further information)
W28.1   Application of internal fixation to bone NEC or **W30.1 Application of external fixation to bone NEC** (if fixation is used, and is not already implicit in the osteotomy code description).
Z site code (where this adds further information)
Z94.-   Laterality of operation

*Code **W15.7 Osteotomy of bone of foot and fixation HFQ** must only be assigned when the metatarsal osteotomy cannot be classified to a site specific code in category **W15.-**. If a site specific code is available in category **W15.-**, use the site specific code with code **W28.1** or **W30.1**, a Z site code and **Z94.-**.

Osteotomy/ osteotomies of phalanx, specified method

For osteotomy/ osteotomies of a phalanx, where the method of osteotomy is specified the following codes must be assigned. The OPCS-4 Alphabetical Index must be used to assign the appropriate osteotomy code:

W12.-   Angulation periarticular division of bone or **W13.- Other periarticular division of bone** or **W14.- Diaphyseal division of bone** or **W15.6 Cuneiform osteotomy of proximal phalanx with resection of head of first metatarsal** or **W77.5 Periarticular osteotomy for stabilisation of joint**
Z Site code (where this adds further information)
W28.1   Application of internal fixation to bone NEC or **W30.1 Application of external fixation to bone NEC** (if fixation is used, and it is not already implicit in the osteotomy code description)
Z Site code (where this adds further information)
Z94.-   Laterality of operation

Osteotomy of phalanx, other specified method or unspecified method

Where phalangeal osteotomy is performed and the method specified is not classifiable to one of the categories listed above, assign the following codes:

W15.7   Osteotomy of bone of foot and fixation HFQ (if with fixation) or **W15.8 Other specified other division of bone** (if without fixation)
Z site code (where this adds further information)
Z94.-   Laterality of operation

Examples:

Displacement osteotomy of head of 2nd metatarsal bone with internal fixation and osteotomy of 1st metatarsal bone with internal fixation, right foot.

W03.6   Osteotomy of multiple metatarsals and fixation HFQ
Z80.1   First metatarsal
Z80.2   Metatarsal NEC
Z94.2   Right sided operation

Osteotomy with fixation was performed on multiple metatarsals of the right foot.

Displacement osteotomy of second metatarsal, right foot.

> **W13.2** **Displacement osteotomy**
> **Z80.2** **Metatarsal NEC**
> **Z94.2** **Right sided operation**

The specified method of osteotomy has been documented.

Scarf osteotomy of 1st metatarsal bone, internal fixation with two screws and Akin osteotomy of 1st proximal phalanx, fixation with one screw, left foot.

> **W15.3** **Osteotomy of first metatarsal bone NEC**
> **W28.1** **Application of internal fixation to bone NEC**
> **Z80.1** **First metatarsal**
> **W15.7** **Osteotomy of bone of foot and fixation HFQ**
> **Z80.3** **Phalanx of great toe**
> **Z94.3** **Left sided operation**

Osteotomy was performed on a single metatarsal and a phalanx, both of the left foot. The osteotomy methods were not stated, only the eponyms were used.

Closing wedge osteotomy of left proximal phalanx of the great toe, internal fixation with a screw.

> **W13.3** **Cuneiform osteotomy NEC**
> **Z80.3** **Phalanx of great toe**
> **W28.1** **Application of internal fixation to bone NEC**
> **Z80.3** **Phalanx of great toe**
> **Z94.3** **Left sided operation**

The term *'ossicle'* at code **W08.7 Excision of accessory ossicle** pertains to a small bone and NOT to operations on the ossicles found in the middle ear which are classified within Chapter D.

PCSW1: Secondary reduction and remanipulation of fracture and fracture dislocation

Secondary reduction and remanipulation of fracture / fracture dislocation codes must only be assigned when the patient undergoes further **reduction** or **remanipulation** on the **same** fracture / fracture dislocation site.

The secondary reduction/ remanipulation procedure may be the **same** or **differ** from the original procedure. These may be:

- The **same**, for example – primary **open** reduction followed by further **open** reduction

  or

- **Different**, for example – primary **closed** reduction followed by subsequent **open** reduction, or reduction without fixation followed by secondary reduction with fixation.

Secondary reductions may be performed in a different health facility to the one that the primary reduction was performed in. The primary reduction may have taken place within the A&E department.

Examples:

Patient admitted with fracture of the right lateral malleolus. A closed reduction of the fracture was performed in A&E and a POP cast was applied. The patient went on to have an open reduction and fixation of the right lateral malleolus fracture using extramedullary plate a few days later.

Codes and sequence for the open reduction and fixation of the right lateral malleolus fracture using extramedullary plate are:

> **W23.2** **Secondary open reduction of fracture of bone and extramedullary fixation HFQ**
> **Z78.4** **Lateral malleolus**

Z94.2   Right sided operation

Patient seen in A&E with fracture of the left distal radius. The patient was treated conservatively with an arm splint. An open reduction and extramedullary fixation using a plate was performed the following morning.

Codes and sequence for the open reduction and fixation of the left distal radius using extramedullary plate are:

W20.1   Primary open reduction of fracture of long bone and extramedullary fixation using plate NEC
Z70.5   Lower end of radius NEC
Z94.3   Left sided operation

Patient has a fracture of the right radius shaft. A closed reduction of the fracture is initially performed in A&E and a POP applied. Six days later the patient is admitted as the fracture has slipped. A further closed reduction is performed under image intensifier.

Codes and sequence for the further closed reduction under image intensifier are:

W26.4   Remanipulation of fracture of bone NEC
Y53.5   Approach to organ under image intensifier
Z70.3   Shaft of radius NEC
Z94.2   Right sided operation

Patient has a fracture of the right radius shaft. The fracture is initially reduced under image intensifier and a POP applied. Six days later the patient is re-admitted as the fracture has slipped. A remanipulation is performed under image intensifier using screw and plate fixation.

O17.6   Remanipulation of fracture of bone and fixation using plate
Y53.5   Approach to organ under image intensifier
Z70.3   Shaft of radius NEC
Z94.2   Right sided operation

PCSW2: Tension band wiring of patella (W21.4)

Tension band wiring of the patella is coded as follows:

W21.4   Primary intra-articular fixation of intra-articular fracture of bone NEC
Z78.7   Patella

Code **W28.4 Insertion of intramedullary fixation and cementing of bone** will primarily be used in the treatment of bone tumours.

PCSW3: Harvest of bone marrow for autologous transplant (W35.8)

The harvest of bone marrow for an autologous transplant is coded as follows:

W35.8   Other specified therapeutic puncture of bone
Y66.7   Harvest of bone marrow
Y70.3   First stage of staged operations NOC
Z75.3   Wing of ilium or **Z74.2 Sternum NEC**

See also PGCS12: Coding grafts and harvest of sites other than skin.

PCSW4: Total hip replacement with acetabular bone graft (W37-W39)

Bone chippings, produced from bone reamed from the patient's acetabulum or femur during a **primary total hip replacement** that are used to **fill defects and secure** the prosthetic joint replacement, must not be coded in addition to the prosthetic joint replacement code(s).

If during a **primary** or **revisional total hip replacement**, an acetabular or femoral bone graft, using either morcellised bone or block of bone, is performed in addition to the joint replacement the following codes must be assigned:

> Primary or revisional total prosthetic replacement of hip joint code
> **W31.-** **Other autograft of bone** or **W32.- Other graft of bone**
> **Z75.6** **Acetabulum** or **Z76.- Femur**
> **Y66.-** **Harvest of bone** (only if an autograft was used)
> Z site code of the harvest (if not identified in the code from **Y66.-**)
> **Z94.-** **Laterality of operation**

Any uncertainty as to whether the joint replacement involves a bone graft, or a packing using bone chippings, must be referred back to the responsible consultant for clarification.

This is an exception to standard **PGCS12: Coding grafts and harvests of sites other than skin**.

Examples:

Primary uncemented left total hip replacement, the defects around the implant were packed using bone chippings from the reamed bone of the patient's acetabulum:

> **W38.1** **Primary total prosthetic replacement of hip joint not using cement**
> **Z94.3** **Left sided operation**

Revisional uncemented left total hip replacement with morcellised autograft of bone to fill large acetabular defect. Bone harvested from left iliac crest.

> **W38.3** **Revision of total prosthetic replacement of hip joint not using cement**
> **W31.4** **Cancellous chip autograft of bone**
> **Z75.6** **Acetabulum**
> **Y66.3** **Harvest of bone from iliac crest**
> **Z94.3** **Left sided operation**

PCSW5: Replacement of infected prosthetic joint replacement

For the **first stage** of the procedure assign the following codes:

> Attention to prosthetic replacement of relevant joint NEC
> **Y03.7   Removal of prosthesis from organ NOC**
> **W81.7   Insertion of therapeutic spacer into joint**
> **Y70.3   First stage of staged operations NOC**
> Z site code
> **Z94.-   Laterality of operation**

Debridement must not be coded in addition when a joint spacer has been inserted following removal of the prosthesis.

For the **second stage** of the procedure assign the following codes:

Insertion of like for like prosthesis:

> Revision of prosthetic replacement of relevant joint code
> **Y71.1   Subsequent stage of staged operations NOC**

Insertion of a different type of prosthesis:

> Conversion to prosthetic replacement of relevant joint code (new prosthesis inserted during this stage)
> Code that classifies conversion from prosthetic replacement of relevant joint (prosthesis removed in stage 1)
> **Y71.1   Subsequent stage of staged operations NOC**

See also PGCS16: Conversion procedures.

The removal of the joint spacer during the second stage of the procedure must not be coded in addition.

Infected prosthetic joint replacements are commonly treated in two stages.

First the prosthesis is removed, surrounding infected tissue is debrided and an antibiotic 'joint spacer' is inserted.

After the infection has cleared the joint spacer is removed and the new joint prosthesis is inserted, the new prosthesis may be the same type, 'like for like', (for example, cemented to cemented) or a different type (for example, cemented to uncemented) to the prosthesis that was removed during the first stage.

There are no dedicated codes for the removal of prosthetic joint replacements, therefore the relevant 'attention to' codes must be used for the first stage. However, as 'revision' and 'conversion to' codes are available within specific joint replacement categories these are used for the second stage when a new joint replacement is inserted.

Examples:

A patient with an infected left cemented total knee replacement is admitted for the first stage of a two stage replacement. The infected joint replacement is removed. The joint is debrided and a joint spacer is inserted. 6 weeks later they are readmitted for the second stage of the procedure. The joint spacer is removed and a new cemented total knee replacement is inserted:

First stage:

> **W42.4   Attention to total prosthetic replacement of knee joint NEC**
> **Y03.7   Removal of prosthesis from organ NOC**
> **W81.7   Insertion of therapeutic spacer into joint**
> **Y70.3   First stage of staged operations NOC**
> **Z84.6   Knee joint**
> **Z94.3   Left sided operation**

Second stage:

> **W40.3**   Revision of total prosthetic replacement of knee joint using cement
> **Y71.1**   Subsequent stage of staged operations NOC
> **Z94.3**   Left sided operation

A patient with an infected left cemented total hip replacement is admitted for the first stage of a two stage replacement. The infected joint replacement is removed. The joint is debrided and a joint spacer is inserted. 4 weeks later they are readmitted for the second stage of the procedure. The joint spacer is removed and a new uncemented total hip replacement is inserted:

First stage:

> **W39.4**   Attention to total prosthetic replacement of hip joint NEC
> **Y03.7**   Removal of prosthesis from organ NOC
> **W81.7**   Insertion of therapeutic spacer into joint
> **Y70.3**   First stage of staged operations NOC
> **Z84.3**   Hip joint
> **Z94.3**   Left sided operation

Second stage:

> **W38.2**   Conversion to total prosthetic replacement of hip joint not using cement
>   ***Note: Use a subsidiary conversion from code as necessary***
> **W37.0**   Conversion from previous cemented total prosthetic replacement of hip joint
> **Y71.1**   Subsequent stage of staged operations NOC
> **Z94.3**   Left sided operation

PCSW6: Unicompartmental knee replacement (W58.1)

Unicompartmental knee replacements are coded as follows:

> **W58.1**   Primary resurfacing arthroplasty of joint
> **Z84.4**   Patellofemoral joint or Z84.5 Tibiofemoral joint (depending on which surfaces were replaced)
> **Z94.-**   Laterality of operation

PCSW13: Patella resurfacing/patella button (W58.1)

When coding patella resurfacing, also known as a patella button procedure, the following codes must be assigned:

> **W58.1**   Primary resurfacing arthroplasty of joint
> **Z78.7**   Patella
> **Z94.-**   Laterality of operation

When patella resurfacing/patella button procedure is performed at the same time as a knee joint replacement, these codes must be assigned after the code(s) for the knee joint replacement.

PCSW7: Ozaki procedure (W76.1)

The Ozaki procedure performed using an open approach is coded as follows:

W76.1 **Excision of ligament**
Z89.1 **Shoulder NEC**

The Ozaki procedure performed using an arthroscopic approach is coded as follows:

W76.1 **Excision of ligament**
Y76.7 **Arthroscopic approach to joint**
Z89.1 **Shoulder NEC**

Release of tennis elbow (T69 or W78)

See PCST1: Release of tennis elbow (T69 or W78)

PCSW8: Autologous chondrocyte implantation into knee joint

The first stage of autologous chondrocyte implantation (ACI) into the knee, when the chondrocytes are harvested, is coded using the following codes:

W89.2 **Endoscopic harvest of autologous chondrocytes**
Y70.3 **First stage of staged operations NOC**
Z site code
Z94.- **Laterality of operation**

The second stage is coded as follows:

Using an open approach:

W71.4 **Open autologous chrondrocyte implantation into articular structure**
Y71.1 **Subsequent stage of staged operations NOC**
Z site code
Z94.- **Laterality of operation**

Using an arthroscopic approach:

W85.3 **Endoscopic autologous chondrocyte implantation of knee joint**
Y71.1 **Subsequent stage of staged operations NOC**
Z94.- **Laterality of operation**

Semilunar cartilage is only found in the knee joint, so is not necessary to assign a site code with codes in category **W82 Therapeutic endoscopic operations on semilunar cartilage**.

PCSW9: Aspiration of prosthetic joint (W90.1)

The aspiration of a prosthetic joint is coded as follows:

> **W90.1 Aspiration of joint**
> **Y53.-   Approach to organ under image control (if used)**
> Z site code
> **Z94.-   Laterality of operation**

These procedures must not be coded using the 'attention to' prosthetic joint replacement procedure codes.

It is not appropriate to assign an 'attention to' code for the aspiration of a prosthetic joint. The presence of the prosthesis may be connected to the need for aspiration; however the aspiration is performed on the cavity of the joint, and does not involve the actual physical parts of the prosthesis.

PCSW10: Acromioclavicular joint excision/decompression with subacromial decompression/acromioplasty

Open acromioclavicular joint (ACJ) excision/decompression is classified using the following codes:

> **W57.2 Primary excision arthroplasty of joint NEC**
> **Z81.2 Acromioclavicular joint**

Arthroscopic ACJ excision/decompression is classified using the following codes:

> **W84.4 Endoscopic decompression of joint**
> **Z81.2 Acromioclavicular joint**

If ACJ excision/decompression and subacromial decompression/acromioplasty (**O29.1 Subacromial decompression**) are performed then both procedures must be coded. If repair of the rotator cuff muscle (**T79.- Repair of muscle**) is performed in addition to either of these procedures then this must also be coded.

Examples:

Arthroscopic acromioplasty with excision (decompression) of arthritic AC joint right shoulder

> **O29.1 Subacromial decompression**
> *Includes: Acromioplasty NEC*
> ***Note: Use a subsidiary code for minimal access approach (Y74–Y76)***
> **Y76.7 Arthroscopic approach to joint**
> **W84.4 Endoscopic decompression of joint**
> **Z81.2 Acromioclavicular joint**
> **Z94.2 Right sided operation**

Open SAD with AC joint excision arthroplasty right shoulder

> **O29.1 Subacromial decompression**
> *Includes: Acromioplasty NEC*
> **W57.2 Primary excision arthroplasty of joint NEC**
> **Z81.2 Acromioclavicular joint**
> **Z94.2 Right sided operation**

Right Arthroscopic SAD with repair of multiple tears of rotator cuff

> **O29.1 Subacromial decompression**
> *Includes: Acromioplasty NEC*
> ***Note: Use a subsidiary code for minimal access approach (Y74–Y76)***
> **Y76.7 Arthroscopic approach to joint**

T79.4   **Plastic repair of multiple tears of rotator cuff of shoulder**
Y76.7   **Arthroscopic approach to joint**
Z94.2   **Right sided operation**

PCSW11: Hybrid knee replacement (O18.-)

Hybrid knee replacements are coded as follows:

O18.1   **Primary hybrid prosthetic replacement of knee joint using cement**
Z77.1   **Condyle of tibia or Z76.5 Lower end of femur NEC** (depending on the component that is cemented)
Z94.-   **Laterality of operation**

Usually, a hybrid knee replacement has a cemented tibial component and an uncemented femoral component. However it is possible to have a hybrid knee replacement with a cemented femoral component and an uncemented tibial component.

Category **O32 Total prosthetic replacement of ankle joint** classifies all total prosthetic replacement of ankle joint whether cemented, uncemented or unspecified.

CHAPTER X
Miscellaneous Operations
(X01–X98)

Chapter standards and guidance

Coding procedures performed for the correction of congenital deformities

See PGCS11: Coding procedures performed for the correction of congenital deformities

Coding standards and guidance

PCSX1: Reamputation (X12.1)

Re-amputations through the same bone as the original amputation at a higher level must be coded as follows:

> **X12.1   Reamputation at higher level**
> Z site code for the bone the reamputation was performed on
> **Z94.-   Laterality of operation**

If the re-amputation involves a different bone to the bone that was originally amputated then this must be coded as an amputation of that bone.

Examples:

Patient has previously undergone a right above knee amputation (AKA). The stump becomes infected and a further three inches of the femoral shaft are amputated.

> **X12.1   Reamputation at higher level**
> **Z76.4   Shaft of femur**
> **Z94.2   Right sided operation**

Patient has previously undergone a right below knee amputation (BKA) due to necrosis of the foot. Following amputation the necrosis reoccurs in the leg and a further amputation is performed above the knee. Codes for the further amputation above the knee:

> **X09.3   Amputation of leg above knee**
> **Z94.2   Right sided operation**

PCSX2: Intravenous infusions and intravenous injections

Intravenous (IV) infusions and IV injections must **only** be coded if the patient is admitted solely for administration of the IV infusion or injection.

The exception is the administration of Streptokinase, *see PCSX3: Administration of Streptokinase*.

Example:

Patient being treated for epilepsy develops a chest infection during the hospital provider spell and is administered IV antibiotics.

> No OPCS-4 code is assigned as the patient was not admitted solely for administration of the IV antibiotics.

PCSX3: Administration of Streptokinase

Whenever the fibrinolytic Streptokinase (clot busting drug) is administered this must be coded according to the method of administration.

The exception is fibrinolytic (clot busting) drugs on the National Tariff High Cost Drugs List.

See the High Cost Drugs Clinical Coding Standards and Guidance- OPCS-4. The list, standards and guidance can be downloaded from the Main Publications page on Delen.

See also PRule 10: National Tariff High Cost Drugs List.

Anti-D injection following delivery (X30.1)

See PCSR8: Anti-D injection following delivery (X30.1).

PCSX4: Blood transfusions (X33)

Only if the patient is admitted solely for the purpose of a blood transfusion(**X33**) must the transfusion be coded. Blood transfusions given during surgery, e.g. major bowel surgery, transplants, joint replacements etc must not be coded.

*The exceptions are **PCSX5: Intraoperative blood salvage and transfusion (X33.7 and X36.4) and X33.4-X33.6 in PCSX8: Bone marrow transplantation and peripheral blood stem cell transplantation.***

PCSX5: Intraoperative blood salvage and transfusion (X33.7 and X36.4)

Code **X36.4 Autologous blood salvage** must only be used in a secondary position.

When intraoperative blood (cell) salvage and reinfusion of the salvaged blood cells into the patient has been performed during a procedure, the following codes must be assigned in addition to the code(s) classifying the procedure during which the cells were salvaged:

> **X36.4   Autologous blood salvage**
> **X33.7   Autologous transfusion of red blood cells**

Where intraoperative blood (cell) salvage has been performed during a procedure and the salvaged blood has not been reinfused during the procedure, the following code must be assigned in addition to the code(s) classifying the procedure during which the cells were salvaged:

> **X36.4   Autologous blood salvage**

Where reinfusion of salvaged blood has been performed after the procedure when intraoperative blood (cell) salvage was performed, the following code must be assigned:

> **X33.7   Autologous transfusion of red blood cells**

*This is an exception to the standard to only code blood transfusions if the patient is admitted solely for the purpose of the blood transfusion in **PCSX4: Blood transfusions.***

PCSX6: Intravenous induction of labour (X35.1)

Code **X35.1 Intravenous induction of labour** must never be used. Codes within Chapter R categories **R14 Surgical induction of labour** and **R15 Other induction of labour** must be used to code induction of labour.

PCSX7: Red Cell Survival procedure (X35.8)

Red Cell Survival procedure must be coded using:

X35.8   Other specified other intravenous injection

Diagnostic blood tests (X36.3, X36.8, X36.9 and U32.1)

See PCSU6: Diagnostic blood tests (U32.1, X36.3, X36.8 and X36.9).

PCSX8: Bone marrow transplantation and peripheral blood stem cell transplantation

Bone marrow harvest and transplantations must be coded as follows:

- Harvest of allogeneic or syngeneic bone marrow (bone marrow taken from the recipient's twin, sibling, parent or an unrelated donor):

    X46.1   Donation of bone marrow
    Z75.3   Wing of ilium or **Z74.2 Sternum NEC** (depending on site of harvest)

- Harvest of autologous bone marrow (bone marrow taken from the recipient):

    W35.8   Other specified therapeutic puncture of bone
    Y66.7   Harvest of bone marrow
    Y70.3   First stage of staged operations NOC
    Z75.3   Wing of ilium or **Z74.2 Sternum NEC** (depending on site of harvest)

- A code from category W34 Graft of bone marrow would be assigned on the episode of care in which the bone marrow was transplanted into the recipient patient – See *PGCS12: Coding grafts and harvest of sites other than skin*.

Peripheral blood stem cells (PBSC) harvest and transplantation must be coded as follows:

- Harvest of allogeneic or syngeneic peripheral blood stem cells (peripheral blood stem cells taken from the recipient's twin, sibling, parent or an unrelated donor):

    X36.1   Blood donation
    Y69.8   Other specified harvest of other tissue

- Harvest of autologous peripheral blood stem cells (peripheral blood stem cells taken from the recipient), when performed during a separate consultant episode to the transplantation:

    X36.1   Blood donation
    Y69.8   Other specified harvest of other tissue
    Y70.3   First stage of staged operations NOC

- A code from **X33.4 Autologous peripheral blood stem cell transplant**, **X33.5 Syngeneic peripheral blood stem cell transplant** or **X33.6 Allogeneic peripheral blood stem cell transplant** plus **Y99.- Donor status** (where doing so adds further information), plus **Y71.1 Subsequent stage of staged operation NOC** would be assigned on the episode of care in which the peripheral blood stem cells were transplanted into the recipient patient – *See also PCSY12: Donor status (Y99)*.

- If the autologous peripheral blood stem cells are harvested and transplanted during the same consultant episode:

    X33.4   Autologous peripheral blood stem cell transplant

This is an exception to the standards to only code blood transfusions if the patient is admitted solely for the purpose of the blood transfusion in PCSX4: Blood transfusions (X33).

PCSX8: *continued*

In **autologous transplants** patients receive their own stem cells.

In **syngeneic transplants** patients receive stem cells from their **identical** twin.

In **allogeneic transplants** (where 'allogeneic' means 'coming from the same species but genetically dissimilar'), patients can receive stem cells from their brother or sister (which would include non-identical twins) or parent. Cells from a person who is not related to the patient (an unrelated donor) may also be used.

PCSX9: Compensation for renal failure (X40)

A code from category **X40 Compensation for renal failure** must be assigned every time an intervention classified to this category is performed. Any procedure(s) performed in order to carry out a procedure classifiable to category **X40**, such as insertion of dialysis catheters, central venous catheters, arteriovenous shunts, etc. must also be coded, with the code from **X40** being sequenced after these other procedures.

PCSX10: Administration of vaccine (X44)

Codes in category **X44 Administration of vaccine** must only be assigned if the patient is admitted solely for the purpose of vaccination.

PCSX11: Donation of organ (X45)

The donation of organs must only to be coded, using a code from category **X45 Donation of organ**, if the patient donating the organs is alive.

The removal of organs for donation from 'brain dead' or 'deceased' patients must not be coded.

PCSX12: Donation of skin (X46.2)

Donation of skin is coded as follows:

> **X46.2   Donation of skin**
> Y harvest code
> Site and laterality code (if necessary)

See PCSS3: Coding of skin grafts and harvests.

Example:

Donation of random pattern flap of skin from back

> **X46.2   Donation of skin**
> **Y56.2   Harvest of random pattern flap of skin from back**

PCSX13: Low-density lipoprotein apheresis (X47.1)

X47.1 Low-density lipoprotein apheresis must be coded each time it is carried out.

PCSX14: Advanced cardiac pulmonary resuscitation (X50.3)

X50.3 Advanced cardiac pulmonary resuscitation must be coded every time it has been performed.

PCSX15: Evaluation of cardioverter defibrillator (X50.5)

Code **X50.5 Evaluation of cardioverter defibrillator** must <u>not</u> be assigned when evaluation/testing is performed during the insertion of the cardioverter defibrillator.

PCSX16: Extracorporeal membrane oxygenation (X58.1)

X58.1 Extracorporeal membrane oxygenation must be coded every time it has been performed.

PCSX17: Anaesthetic without surgery (X59)

Codes in category **X59 Anaesthetic without surgery** are used to code patients who are anaesthetised, but who do not subsequently undergo the procedure they were anaesthetised for. The type of anaesthetic given may be coded in addition if this information is required to be collected locally. *See PCSY10: Anaesthetic (Y80–Y84).*

Example:

Lumbar epidural anaesthetic, no other procedure performed

> **X59.8   Other specified anaesthetic without surgery**
> **Y81.1   Epidural anaesthetic using lumbar approach**

PCSX18: Rehabilitation Assessment (X60)

When an assessment for rehabilitation, accompanied by a written report, is carried out by a **team from two or more clinical professions within local therapy/support services** assign:

> **X60.1   Rehabilitation assessment by multidisciplinary non-specialised team**

When an assessment for rehabilitation, accompanied by a written report, is carried out by a **team from two or more clinical professions within district specialist service(s)** assign:

> **X60.2   Rehabilitation assessment by multidisciplinary specialised team**

When an assessment for rehabilitation, accompanied by a written report, is carried out by a **team (or individual) from a single clinical profession within local therapy/support services** assign:

> **X60.3   Rehabilitation assessment by unidisciplinary non-specialised team**

When an assessment for rehabilitation, accompanied by a written report, is carried out by a **team (or individual) from a single clinical profession within district specialist service(s)** assign:

> **X60.4   Rehabilitation assessment by unidisciplinary specialised team**

See PCSU7: Rehabilitation (U50-U54) – Where a patient receives rehabilitation assessment (**X60**) and actual rehabilitation (**U50–U54**) within the *same* hospital provider spell, only one code is required from within the range **U50–U54**.

PCSX19: Assessment (X62)

The codes at category **X62 Assessment** must only be used in an outpatient setting.

PCSX20: Radiotherapy (X65, X67–X68)

Preparation for radiotherapy

Preparation for radiotherapy is coded as follows:

> **X67.-   Preparation for external beam radiotherapy** or **X68 Preparation for brachytherapy**
> **Y92.-   Support for preparation for radiotherapy** (if used)

Code **Y92.1 Technical support for preparation for radiotherapy** includes the manufacture of patient specific devices generally undertaken in the 'mould' room. These are typically immobilisation devices such as impression and shell fitting, lead cut-outs, mouth bites and beam shaping devices.

PCSX20: *continued*

Preparation codes must:

- be used for **both** inpatient and outpatient activity

- only be assigned **once** to cover **all** planning for each prescription regardless of the number required for completion of the preparation process

- be assigned on the first attendance/episode for delivery of radiotherapy

- be sequenced before the delivery codes.

Delivery of radiotherapy

Radiotherapy delivery is coded using the following methods:

Coding radiotherapy delivery using body system chapter codes

Where a body system chapter code that classifies radiotherapy is available (e.g. **A61.3 Radiotherapy to lesion of peripheral nerve**) this must be used as follows:

A-W	Body system chapter radiotherapy code
X65.-	**Radiotherapy delivery**
Y35.-	**Introduction of removable radioactive material into organ NOC** or
Y36.-	**Introduction of non-removable material into organ NOC** or
Y91.-	**External beam radiotherapy**

(a code from **Y89.- Brachytherapy** is assigned with **Y35.-** or **Y36.-** if applicable)

Y53.-	**Approach to organ under image control** (if used)
Y80.-	**General anaesthetic** (if radiotherapy was delivered under anaesthetic).

Coding radiotherapy delivery using codes from Chapter X

Where a body system code is not available, the following codes and sequence must be applied:

X65.-	**Radiotherapy delivery**
Y35.-	**Introduction of removable radioactive material into organ NOC** or
Y36.-	**Introduction of non-removable material into organ NOC** or
Y91.-	**External beam radiotherapy**

(a code from **Y89.- Brachytherapy** is assigned with **Y35.-** or **Y36.-** if applicable)

Y53.-	**Approach to organ under image control** (if used)
Y80.-	**General anaesthetic** (if radiotherapy was delivered under anaesthetic)
	Z site code (to identify the area being treated by the radiotherapy).

When coding radiotherapy delivery:

- Code **X65.9 Unspecified radiotherapy delivery** must only be used when the method of radiotherapy delivery is not classifiable to any of the other fourth-characters within the category. An additional code from category **Y91 External beam radiotherapy** must NOT be assigned with code **X65.9**

- For outpatients and daycases, radiotherapy delivery **must** be coded every time a fraction is given

- For inpatients, radiotherapy delivery must only be coded once per hospital provider spell, regardless of the number of fractions.

Codes **X65.5 Oral delivery of radiotherapy for thyroid ablation** and **X65.7 Delivery of radionuclide therapy NEC** do not require the addition of a code from categories **Y35**, **Y36**, **Y89**, or **Y91**.

PCSX20: *continued*

See also:

- *PCSJ1: Selective internal radiotherapy (SIRT) of liver using microspheres (J12.3)*
- *PCSM9: Radioactive seed implantation into prostate (M70.6).*

A prescription specifies a dose and fractionation for a series of identical treatments. This is similar to a medical prescription. Different anatomical sites treated concurrently would have separate prescriptions.

Codes within category **X67 Preparation for external beam radiotherapy** are divided into 'simple' and 'complex'. Clinical Coding Departments must liaise with clinical staff to determine what actual techniques would fall into these two categories, but for information purposes the following advice is given:

Simple radiotherapy is a standard technique with standard imaging and dosimetry. It would probably include techniques such as:

- Single direct field

- Parallel opposed (two fields opposite each other)

- 3-field technique (three individual fields all incident on the same tumour volume)

- 4-field Box (in effect two sets of parallel opposed fields incident on the same tumour volume).

These techniques are relatively easy to plan and the dosimetry is straight-forward. Any deviations from this standard planning protocol may fall into the complex subcategory because they will be out of the norm, need more consideration and be more time-consuming on the part of the dosimetrist.

Complex radiotherapy planning involves more complicated techniques requiring more time and thought from the dosimetrist, and will probably involve more detailed imaging and field placement:

- Intensity Modulated Radiotherapy (IMRT) for external radiotherapy only

- Conformal therapy techniques

- Half and Total Body Irradiation (TBI)

- Multi-phase techniques

- Probably all brachytherapy techniques, as the dosimetry involved is usually quite sophisticated.

Stereotactic radiation therapy is a specialized type of external beam radiotherapy. It is divided into two types:

- Stereotactic radiosurgery (SRS) single or several stereotactic radiation treatments of the brain or spine

- Stereotactic body radiation therapy (SBRT) one or several stereotactic radiation treatments within the body (excluding brain or spine)

Stereotactic radiation may be delivered by a number of different devices/machines. Brand names should not be confused with the actual type of stereotactic radiation.

High dose rate brachytherapy is delivered through temporarily placed applicators in a shielded room. Multiple fractions may be given and patients may attend the unit more than once in a day.

Pulsed dose rate brachytherapy is delivered through temporarily placed applicators, however the radiation dose is given over many hours in short pulses. The patient will remain in a shielded room for the duration of the delivery.

Examples:

Preparation and delivery of pulsed dose brachytherapy therapy for prostate cancer

X68.3	**Preparation for interstitial brachytherapy**
M71.2	**Implantation of radioactive substance into prostate**
X65.3	**Delivery of a fraction of interstitial radiotherapy**

> *Note: Use a subsidiary code to identify introduction of radioactive material (Y35, Y36)*

> *Note: Use a subsidiary code to identify brachytherapy (Y89)*

Y35.4	**Introduction of radioactive substance into organ for brachytherapy NOC**
Y89.2	**Pulsed dose rate brachytherapy treatment**

Preparation and delivery of percutaneous intraluminal brachytherapy (using removable radioactive material) to bile duct cholangiocarcinoma using fluoroscopic control

X68.1	**Preparation for intraluminal brachytherapy**
J48.7	**Percutaneous brachytherapy of lesion of bile duct**

> *Note: Use an additional code to specify radiotherapy delivery (X65)*

> *Note: Use a subsidiary code to identify method of image control (Y53)*

X65.6	**Delivery of a fraction of intraluminal brachytherapy**

> *Note: Use a subsidiary code to identify introduction of radioactive material (Y35, Y36)*

Y35.4	**Introduction of radioactive substance into organ for brachytherapy NOC**
Y53.4	**Approach to organ under fluoroscopic control**

Preparation and delivery of external beam radiotherapy to lesion of peripheral nerve

X67.-	**Preparation for external beam radiotherapy**
A61.3	**Radiotherapy to lesion of peripheral nerve**

> *Note: Use an additional code to specify radiotherapy delivery (X65)*

X65.4	**Delivery of a fraction of external beam radiotherapy NEC**

> *Note: Use a subsidiary code to identify external beam radiotherapy (Y91)*

Y91.9	**Unspecified external beam radiotherapy**

Simple preparation using imaging and dosimetry and delivery of simple external beam radiotherapy for adenocarcinoma of prostate using linear accelerator (megavoltage machine)

X67.4	**Preparation for simple radiotherapy with imaging and dosimetry**
X65.4	**Delivery of a fraction of external beam radiotherapy NEC**

> *Note: Use a subsidiary code to identify external beam radiotherapy (Y91)*

Y91.2	**Megavoltage treatment for simple radiotherapy**
Z42.2	**Prostate**

Preparation and delivery of hypofractionated stereotactic external beam radiotherapy to lesion of lung

X67.-	**Preparation for external beam radiotherapy**
X65.4	**Delivery of a fraction of external beam radiotherapy NEC**

> *Note: Use a subsidiary code to identify external beam radiotherapy (Y91)*

Y91.5	**Megavoltage treatment for hypofractionated sterotactic radiotherapy**
Z24.6	**Lung**

PCSX21: Procurement and delivery of drugs for chemotherapy for neoplasm (X70–X74)

When the route of chemotherapy delivery is intravesical, intrathecal or intracavitary, a body system chapter code identifying the route of delivery must be assigned in addition to the chemotherapy code(s) from categories **X70–X74**. The body system code must be sequenced before the code(s) from **X70-X74**.

Codes in categories **X70–X74** must only be assigned for patients receiving chemotherapy in the treatment of malignant or in-situ neoplasms. When they are used to treat other non-neoplastic conditions, the appropriate high cost drug (HCD) code will be assigned from categories **X81–X98**.

Chemotherapy drugs used for the treatment of non-malignant (non-neoplastic) conditions that are not on the HCD list, must be coded elsewhere e.g. **X35.2 Intravenous chemotherapy, X29.2 Continuous intravenous infusion of therapeutic substance NEC** etc.

See also PRule 11: National Tariff Chemotherapy Regimens List.

For full standards for coding chemotherapy see the DH Chemotherapy Regimens List and Chemotherapy Regimens Clinical Coding Standards and Guidance which can be downloaded from the Main Publications page on Delen.

PCSX22: High Cost Drugs (X81–X98)

Categories **X81–X98** must only be used for the coding of High Cost Drugs (HCD).

Codes classifying high cost drugs must be assigned in preference to other codes in Chapter X which classify method of administration. However if a high cost drug is injected into a specific site classifiable to a body system chapter (such as a sweat gland), then a body system chapter code must be assigned. The body system code must be sequenced before the high cost drug code.

The high cost drugs and specific standards and examples on the use of categories **X81-X98** can be found in the separate **National Tariff High Cost Drugs List and High Cost Drugs Clinical Coding Standards and Guidance – OPCS-4 which can be downloaded from the Main Publications page on** Delen.

See also PRule 10: National Tariff High Cost Drugs List.

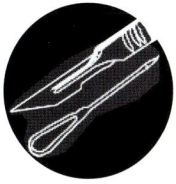

Subsidiary Classification of Methods of Operation
(Y01–Y99)

Chapter standards and guidance

Subsidiary Chapters Y and Z

See PRule 7: Subsidiary Chapters Y and Z

Sequencing of codes in Chapter Y with codes in Chapter Z

See PGCS14: Sequencing of codes in Chapter Y with codes in Chapter Z.

PChSY1: Use of codes in Chapter Y

Codes from Chapter Y are used to enhance codes from the body system chapters where this adds further information about the intervention/procedure that cannot be fully reflected by the assignment of the body system code alone. In many cases a note exists at category or subcategory code level within the main body system chapters indicating that a code from Chapter Y is required, however these codes can also be assigned to codes where one of these notes is not present.

Codes in Chapter Y must only be used in a secondary position following a code from the body system chapters (A–X).

Examples:

Laser therapeutic keratectomy right eye

> **C45.1** **Superficial keratectomy**
> *Includes:* *Laser keratectomy*
> > **Note:** *For laser keratectomy use a subsidiary code to identify laser modification of organ (Y08.5)*
> **Y08.5** **Laser modification of organ NOC**
> **Z94.2** **Right sided operation**

Endoscopic total laser excision of semilunar cartilage of right knee

> **W82.1** **Endoscopic total excision of semilunar cartilage**
> **Y08.1** **Laser excision of organ NOC**
> **Z94.2** **Right sided operation**

Coding standards and guidance

PCSY1: Argon plasma coagulation (Y10.2 and Y17.1)

When coding Argon Plasma Coagulation (APC) codes **Y10.2 Electrocauterisation of organ NOC** or **Y17.1 Electrocauterisation of lesion of organ NOC** must be used in addition to a code that classifies a cauterisation procedure. Where a cauterisation code does not exist, a code for destruction must be used. These codes must **not** be used to classify APC when used as a means of haemostasis at the end of a procedure.

Example:

Fibreoptic endoscopic argon plasma coagulation of lesion of pylorus.

G43.3	**Fibreoptic endoscopic cauterisation of lesion of upper gastrointestinal tract**
Y17.1	**Electrocauterisation of lesion of organ NOC**
Z27.3	**Pylorus**

Electrochemotherapy (Y12.3)

For the standard for coding electrochemotherapy see the National Tariff Chemotherapy Regimens List and Chemotherapy Regimens Clinical Coding Standards and Guidance which can be downloaded from the Main Publications page on Delen.

See also PRule 11: National Tariff Chemotherapy Regimens List.

Radioactive implants (Y35 and Y36)

For the standards when assigning codes in categories Y35 and Y36 for radiotherapy procedures see PCSX20: Radiotherapy (X65, X67-X68).

PCSY2: Insertion of adhesion barrier (Y36.8)

For procedures that include the insertion of an adhesion barrier that prevent the formation of adhesions following surgery the following code must be assigned in addition to the main procedure code:

Y36.8   Other specified introduction of non-removable material into organ NOC

Fluorescence cystoscopy and cystoscopy using photodynamic substance (Y37.1)

See PCSM5: Fluorescence cystoscopy and cystoscopy using photodynamic substance.

PCSY3: Lipofilling (Y39.4)

Code **Y39.4 Lipofilling injection into organ NOC** is to be used as a supplementary code for lipofilling on any area other than the breast.

Example:

Lipofilling of both cheeks. Fat taken from the right inner upper thigh

S62.8	**Other specified other operations on subcutaneous tissue**
Y39.4	**Lipofilling injection into organ NOC**
Z47.3	**Skin of cheek**
	Includes: Subcutaneous tissue of face
Z94.1	**Bilateral operation**
Y67.2	**Harvest of composite of skin and fat**
	Includes: Harvest of dermis fat NEC
Z50.4	**Skin of leg NEC**
	Includes: Subcutaneous tissue of other site
Z94.2	**Right sided operation**

PCSY4: Endoscopic tattooing of lesions (Y39.5)

If during an endoscopy, lesions are marked by tattooing with ink so that they may be positively identified at a later date, code **Y39.5 Tattooing of organ NOC** must be assigned as a supplementary code.

PCSY5: Endoscopic ultrasound staging examination of organ NOC (Y41.2)

When an endoscopic ultrasound examination (EUS) is performed as a staging examination code **Y41.2 Endoscopic ultrasound staging examination of organ NOC** must be assigned in addition to the body system EUS code.

PCSY6: Approach to organ (Y46–Y52 and Y74-Y76)

Where a method of approach classifiable to categories **Y46–Y52 and Y74-Y76** is not incorporated within the body system code description, a code from categories **Y46–Y52 and Y74-Y76** must be assigned directly after the body system code to identify the method of approach. Any site and laterality codes must be assigned after the approach code.

Where a number of procedures have taken place using different methods of approach a code from categories (**Y46–Y52 and Y74-Y76**) must be assigned after each body system code.

See also PGCS1: Endoscopic and minimal access operations that do not have a specific code

The classification recognises the resource differences between alternative methods of approach to certain operations, particularly open and endoscopic procedures.

In many cases, the method of approach is incorporated into the code itself, e.g. **J36.1 Excision of ampulla of Vater using duodenal approach**.

Examples:

Open biopsy of lesion of frontal region of brain through frontal burrhole

> **A04.1** **Open biopsy of lesion of tissue of frontal lobe of brain**
> **Y47.2** **Frontal burrhole approach to contents of cranium**

Thoracoscopic video-assisted biopsy of lesion of lung

> **E59.3** **Biopsy of lesion of lung NEC**
> **Y74.4** **Thoracoscopic video-assisted approach to thoracic cavity**

FESS repair of sphenoid sinus

> **E15.3** **Repair of sphenoidal sinus**
> **Y76.1** **Functional endoscopic sinus surgery**

PCSY7: Approach to organ under image control (Y53 and Y78)

The following applies to codes in categories **Y53 Approach to organ under image control** and **Y78 Arteriotomy approach to organ under image control**:

- When a procedure has been performed using image control and the code that classifies the procedure **does not** state the type of image control used, then a code from these categories **must be** assigned. If the specific method of image control is not stated, the fourth-character **.9** must be assigned

- The code(s) from categories **Y53** or **Y78** must be sequenced after the intervention and before the site and laterality codes

- If the code that classifies the procedure states the type of image control used, a code from categories **Y53** or **Y78** **must not** be assigned. e.g. **L72.6 Intravascular ultrasound of artery NEC** and **Q51.1 Transvaginal ultrasound guided aspiration of ovarian cyst**

- If the type of image control used is implicit in the procedure, i.e. the procedure is always carried out using one specific form of image control, then a code from categories **Y53** or **Y78** **must not** be assigned: e.g. **R37.3 Fetal biometry** which is always carried out using ultrasound.

- If image control has been used before, during or after a procedure as a method of checking the anatomical position, or the position of a prosthesis/fixator after insertion, or to confirm a procedure is complete, a code to classify the image control **must not** be assigned.

Y53 Approach to organ under image control

Codes in category **Y53 Approach to organ under image control** are used as additional codes for any procedure that uses image control that may or may not be performed via percutaneous approach. This excludes those procedures performed using an arteriotomy approach under image control (**Y78**).

- Where a number of different types of image control have been used together a code for each type of image control used must be assigned. The exception to this is fluoroscopy when used with an image intensifier, where it is only necessary to assign code **Y53.4 Approach to organ under fluoroscopic control**.

- *See also PCSY11: Gestational age (Y95).*

Y78 Arteriotomy approach to organ under image control

Codes within category **Y78 Arteriotomy approach to organ under image control** must only be used where it is clear that an arteriotomy approach using image control has been performed. Common terms which indicate an arteriotomy has been performed are: incision into artery, surgical cut-down or cutting of artery.

The arteriotomy will always require closure with either suture or clips to the overlying skin and this must not be coded in addition.

PCSY7: *continued*

The majority of interventions that are undertaken on arteries by radiologists and some surgeons are referred to as Interventional Radiology procedures and are minimally invasive. These are usually undertaken by putting local anaesthetic in the skin and then passing a small needle and tube into the artery without a surgical incision. This is referred to as a percutaneous access and the intervention is classed as a 'percutaneous transluminal' procedure.

Once inside the artery, the radiologist or surgeon needs a means of visualising the artery and this is achieved by using image control.

An arteriotomy is a method of approach used to gain access to the inside of the artery by surgical incision. Most patients having an arteriotomy will have a treatment that does not require image guidance as the surgeon will have a direct view of the artery. However, some interventions, in particular stent grafts for aneurysms, require incision away from the site of the procedure, and therefore require some form of image control to allow precise visualisation.

Examples:

Percutaneous transluminal ablation of ventricular wall under image conrol

K57.6	**Percutaneous transluminal ablation of ventricular wall**
Y53.9	**Unspecified approach to organ under image control**

Percutaneous biopsy of lesion of liver under x-ray (radiological) control

J13.2	**Percutaneous biopsy of lesion of liver NEC**
Y53.1	**Approach to organ under radiological control**

Percutaneous transluminal insertion of one plastic stent into left femoral artery under image control

L63.5	**Percutaneous transluminal insertion of stent into femoral artery**
	Note: Use a supplementary code for placement of stent (L76, L89, O20)
L76.2	**Endovascular placement of one plastic stent**
Y53.9	**Unspecified approach to organ under image control**
Z94.3	**Left sided operation**

Manipulation of fractured right radius under image intensifier

W26.2	**Manipulation of fracture of bone NEC**
Y53.5	**Approach to organ under image intensifier**
Z70.9	**Radius NEC**
Z94.2	**Right sided operation**

Insertion of one endovascular stent graft into infrarenal abdominal aortic aneurysm using fluoroscopic guidance via femoral artery incision

L27.1	**Endovascular insertion of stent graft for infrarenal abdominal aortic aneurysm**
O20.3	**Endovascular placement of one stent graft NEC**
Y78.1	**Arteriotomy approach to organ using image guidance with fluoroscopy**

Insertion of nasogastric feeding tube into stomach; tube position checked with ultrasound to ensure correct siting

G47.8	**Other specified intubation of stomach**

Open reduction of fragment of right scaphoid and screw fixation. The position of the screw was checked using image intensifier

> **W19.5**   **Primary open reduction of fragment of bone and fixation using screw**
> **Z72.2**   **Scaphoid bone**
> **Z94.2**   **Right sided operation**

L4/L5 posterior decompression for spinal stenosis, level checked with x-ray prior to incision

> **V25.5**   **Primary posterior decompression of lumbar spine**
> **V55.1**   **One level of spine**

Coding grafts, harvests and donations

See:

- *PGCS12: Coding grafts and harvests of sites other than skin*
- *PCSS3: Coding skin grafts and harvests*
- *PCSX12: Donation of skin (X46.2)*
- *PCSY12: Donor status (Y99).*

Staged procedures (Y70.3, Y71.1 and Y71.7)

See PGCS18: Staged procedures.

Maintenance and attention to procedures

See PGCS17: Maintenance and attention to procedures.

Temporary operations

See PGCS19: Temporary operations.

Failed percutaneous and minimal access procedures converted to open (Y71.4 and Y71.5)

See PGCS4: Failed percutaneous and minimal access procedures converted to open.

Endoscopic and minimal access operations that do not have a specific code (Y74-Y76)

See PGCS1: Endoscopic and minimal access operations that do not have a specific code.

PCSY8: Cardiopulmonary bypass (Y73.1)

Y73.1 Cardiopulmonary bypass must always be assigned in a secondary position whenever it is stated to have been carried out.

PCSY9: Intraoperative fluid monitoring (Y73.6)

Y73.6 Intraoperative fluid monitoring which includes Oesophageal Doppler Monitoring (ODM) must only be coded once per theatre visit.

PCSY10: Anaesthetic (Y80-Y84)

When radiotherapy is delivered under general anaesthetic, a code from category **Y80 General anaesthetic** must be assigned in addition to the radiotherapy codes, *see PCSX20: Radiotherapy (X65, X67–X68)*.

In all other cases anaesthetics may be recorded if this information is required to be captured locally.

See also PCSX17: Anaesthetic without surgery (X59).

It is regarded as best practice to record epidurals or spinals performed on obstetric patients.

Brachytherapy (Y89), External beam radiotherapy (Y91) and support for preparation for radiotherapy (Y92)

For the standards when assigning codes in categories Y89, Y91 and Y92 for radiotherapy procedures see PCSX20: Radiotherapy (X65, X67-X68).

Gallium-67 imaging (Y93) and Radiopharmaceutical imaging (Y94)

For the standards when assigning codes in categories Y93 or Y94 for nuclear medicine procedures see PCSU3: Nuclear medicine imaging procedures.

PCSY11: Gestational age (Y95)

Codes in category **Y95 Gestational age** must be assigned in a subsidiary position, where this information is available, with various codes in Chapters Q and R as indicated by the ***Notes*** at category and code level.

Where a code from categories **Y95** and **Y53** are both required the code from category **Y53** must be sequenced before the code from **Y95**.

Example:
Percutaneous blood transfusion of 22 week fetus under ultrasonic control

> **R04.3**   **Percutaneous blood transfusion of fetus**
> > *Note: Use a subsidiary code to identify method of image control (Y53)*
> > *Note: Use a subsidiary code to identify gestational age (Y95)*
> **Y53.2**   **Approach to organ under ultrasonic control**
> **Y95.1**   **Over twenty weeks gestational age**

In vitro fertilisation (Y96)

See PCSQ3: In vitro fertilisation (Q13.1, Q21.1 and Q38.3).

Radiological contrast and body areas (Y97-Y98)

See PCSU2: Radiological contrast and body areas (Y97-Y98).

PCSY12: Donor status (Y99)

Codes within category **Y99 Donor status** must only be assigned in addition to the OPCS-4 code which describes the transplantation procedure where they provide additional information that is not stated in the main operation code.

Codes from **Y99** must only be assigned on the recipient's hospital episode and not the donor's episode.

See:

- *PGCS12: Coding grafts and harvests of sites other than skin*
- *PCSX8: Bone marrow transplantation and peripheral stem cell transplantation.*

Example:

Allotransplantion of right kidney from patient's sister

     M01.2   **Allotransplantation of kidney from live donor**
     Y99.2   **Live related donor**
     Z94.2   **Right sided operation**

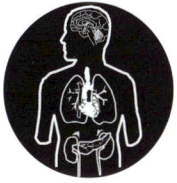

CHAPTER Z
Subsidiary Classification of Sites of Operation
(Z01–Z99, O11–O14, O16, O28, O30-O31, O33)

Chapter standards and guidance

Subsidiary Chapters Y and Z

See PRule 7: Subsidiary Chapters Y and Z

PChSZ1: Use of codes in Chapter Z

Codes from Chapter Z must be used to enhance codes from Chapters A–X where this adds further information about the site and laterality of intervention.

Codes in Chapter Z must only be used in a secondary position following a code from Chapters A–X.

Assigning site codes for endoscopic procedures

See PGCS10: Coding endoscopic procedures for standards for the assignment of site codes when coding endoscopic procedures.

Sequencing of codes in Chapter Y with codes in Chapter Z

See PGCS 14: Sequencing of codes in Chapter Y with codes in Chapter Z.

Coding standards and guidance

PCSZ1: Site codes

Site codes from Chapter Z must always be assigned when this adds further information about the site the procedure was performed on.

A site code is not required when it does not provide any additional information.

For instance where the site of the intervention is already specified within the procedure code description (e.g. **W48.1 Primary prosthetic replacement of head of femur NEC**), or where a site code is not available which further specifies the site or sub site.

See also PChSL2: Assigning codes for specifically classifiable arteries.

Examples:

Repair of right abducens nerve (upper cranial nerve vi)

> **A30.2** **Repair of oculomotor nerve (iii)**
> *Includes: Repair of trochlear nerve (iv)*
> *   Repair of abducens nerve (vi)*
> **Z03.6** **Abducens nerve (vi)**
> **Z94.2** **Right sided operation**

Excision of lesion of upper outer quadrant of right breast

> **B28.3** **Excision of lesion of breast**
> **Z15.2** **Upper outer quadrant of breast**
> **Z94.2** **Right sided operation**

Curettage of lesion of skin of forehead

> **S08.3** **Curettage of lesion of skin of head or neck NEC**
> **Z47.1** **Skin of forehead**

Open reduction and internal fixation (ORIF) of fractured left distal radius using plate

> **W20.1** **Primary open reduction of fracture of long bone and extramedullary fixation using plate NEC**
> **Z70.5** **Lower end of radius NEC**
> **Z94.3** **Left sided operation**

PCSZ2: Laterality of operation (Z94)

When laterality is documented in the medical record, and is not already implicit in the code description, it must be coded.

When multiple procedures are carried out on the same site it is only necessary to assign the laterality code once after all of the procedures on that site, however there is nothing to prohibit the assignment of the laterality code multiple times in such instances, if a Trust has a local need to do so.

Examples:

Bilateral dissection tonsillectomy

> **F34.1** **Bilateral dissection tonsillectomy**

Endoscopic cryoablation of lesion of right kidney, patient previously had their left kidney removed 3 years ago.

> **M10.4** **Endoscopic cryoablation of lesion of kidney**
> **Z94.2** **Right sided operation**

Arthroscopic acromioplasty with excision (decompression) of arthritic AC joint right shoulder

> **O29.1** **Subacromial decompression**
> **Y76.7** **Arthroscopic approach to joint**
> **W84.4** **Endoscopic decompression of joint**
> **Z81.2** **Acromioclavicular joint**
> **Z94.2** **Right sided operation**

Curettage of lesion of right cheek, shave excision of lesion from left external ear and cauterisation of lesion of skin of right buttock

> **S08.3** **Curettage of lesion of skin of head or neck NEC**
> **Z47.3** **Skin of cheek**
> **Z94.2** **Right sided operation**
> **D02.1** **Excision of lesion of external ear**
> **S06.3** **Shave excision of lesion of skin of head or neck**
> **Z94.3** **Left sided operation**
> **S11.1** **Cauterisation of lesion of skin NEC**
> **Z49.5** **Skin of buttock**
> **Z94.2** **Right sided operation**

Primary suture of laceration of skin on the left side of the back

S42.1   Primary suture of skin NEC
Z49.4   Skin of back
Z94.3   Left sided operation

Cauterisation of basal cell carcinoma (BCC) from the skin of the left and right arms

S11.1   Cauterisation of lesion of skin NEC
Z50.1   Skin of arm
Z94.1   Bilateral operation

INDEX OF STANDARDS

SUMMARY OF CHANGES

This section provides notification of all changes to the National Clinical Coding Standards OPCS-4 reference book, for use from 1 April 2018.

Each entry is shown with track changes to indicate what has changed. Deletions appear as strikethrough whilst additions appear underlined. Where part of a standard or guidance has been updated, the whole standard or guidance will be displayed. Where examples are updated, only the example that has been updated will be displayed.

Where appropriate, a rationale is provided to indicate why a standard has been introduced, updated or deleted.

Reference to the Clinical Classifications Service has been updated throughout the reference book to reflect our new name, Terminology and Classifications Delivery Service. Furthermore, links that previously directed users to the Technology Reference Data Update Distribution (TRUD) service have been changed to Delen, except for the cross-maps as these are still available for download via TRUD.

General Coding Standards

PGCS1 has been updated to reflect the changes to **PCSZ2: Laterality of operation (Z94).**

PGCS1: Endoscopic and minimal access operations that do not have a specific code

When an endoscopic or minimally invasive procedure (i.e. arthroscopic, thoracoscopic and laparoscopic) is undertaken but no specific code exists to capture this type of approach, dual coding is required. The following codes and sequencing is required:

- Open procedure code

- **Y74–Y76** minimal access approach code

    o When more than one minimally invasive procedure has been undertaken an approach code must be assigned after each open procedure code

- Chapter Y Subsidiary Classification of Methods of Operation code (if required)

- Chapter Z site code(s)

- **Z94.- Laterality of operation** (if ~~a paired organ~~required)

~~Where more than one procedure is performed on the same anatomical site, the laterality code is only assigned once after all codes assigned to identify the procedure on that site.~~

The Tabular List of the classification includes a range of categories designated as 'endoscopic' procedures, e.g. **M42 Endoscopic extirpation of lesion of bladder.**

When the classification was constructed it was intended that these categories would be primarily used for operations carried out through existing anatomical passages. However, in the past, some of these categories were also expected to be used for operations carried out using minimal incisions through which rigid or fibreoptic scopes are introduced into body cavities, e.g. **Q37 Endoscopic reversal of female sterilisation.**

This practice was maintained in subsequent versions of OPCS-4 and further specific categories were introduced to differentiate between endoscopic and laparoscopic, e.g. **J17.1 Endoscopic ultrasound examination of liver and biopsy of lesion of liver and J09.3 Laparoscopic ultrasound examination of liver NEC.**

The first example in **PGCS6** has been updated to ensure consistency with **PCSB2 Excision of breast with lymph node clearance and breast reconstruction (B27-B29, B38, B39 and B41).**

PGCS6: Radical operations

Example:

Radical mastectomy involving total removal of left breast, both pectoral muscles and block dissection of axillary lymph nodes

> B27.2　Total mastectomy and excision of both pectoral muscles NEC
> > *Note: Use a supplementary code for removal of lymph node (T85–T87)*
>
> ~~Z94.3　Left sided operation~~
> T85.2　Block dissection of axillary lymph nodes
> Z94.3　Left sided operation

PGCS13 has been deleted and **PCSY7** has been updated to cover this standard. References have also been added the Chapter V and Chapter W.

~~PGCS13: Image control used for checking position of reduced fractures and the correct siting of fixators~~

~~When image control has been used merely as a method of checking the position of a reduced fracture, or checking the correct siting of a fixator, then image control **MUST NOT** be recorded. The form of image control must only be recorded if the procedure itself is performed using image control.~~

~~**Example:**~~

~~*Open reduction of fragment of right scaphoid and screw fixation. The position of the screw was checked using image intensifier*~~

> ~~W19.5　Primary open reduction of fragment of bone and fixation using screw~~
> ~~Z72.2　Scaphoid bone~~
> ~~Z94.2　Right sided operation~~

Chapter A Nervous system

PCSA3 has been updated to reflect the changes to **PCSZ2: Laterality of operation (Z94).** An example has also been added to outline that the vagus nerve is part of the peripheral nervous system.

PCSA3: Neurostimulators (A09, A33, A48 and A70)

When a neurostimulator is permanently implanted under the skin the following codes and sequencing are applied:

- Code that classifies the implantation, introduction or insertion of neurostimulator

- Chapter Z site code, where this adds additional information

When electrode leads are implanted temporarily to test whether the intervention is likely to be effective and the pulse generator device is not implanted under the skin the following codes and sequencing are applied:

- Code that classifies insertion of neurostimulator electrodes

- **Y70.5 Temporary operations**

- Chapter Z site code, where this add further information

- **Z94.- laterality of operation** (if ~~the nerves are 'paired'~~ applicable)

Example:

Transcutaneous stimulation of the cervical branch of the vagus nerve:

> **A70.7   Application of transcutaneous electrical nerve stimulator**
> **Z04.4   Vagus nerve (x)**

PCSA7 has been developed to enable a spinal dura repair to be coded to the correct subcategory as the current index trail only directs to a repair of the meninges of the brain.

PCSA7: Repair of spinal dura

Repair of the spinal dura (as opposed to the dura of the brain) must be coded using **A51.8 Other specified other operations on meninges of spinal cord.**

An additional code(s) from **Chapter Y Subsidiary classification of methods of operation** must also be assigned to specify the type of repair where this adds further information and the information is documented within the medical record.

Codes within the range **A38-A43** must not be used to classify procedures on the spinal dura, as these categories classify procedures on the meninges of the brain only.

Chapter K Heart

PCSK6: Ablation of the heart with 3D mapping (K58.6)

Chapter L Arteries and veins

PCSL8 has been moved from the *Coding Clinic March 2017*. It was developed as a result of collaboration between the Terminology and Classifications Delivery Service and the Abdominal aortic aneurysm (AAA) & Thoracoabdominal aortic aneurysm (TAAA) subgroup to support accurate and consistent coding of replacement/repair of aorta for aortic aneurysm and aortic dissection.

PCSL8: Replacement/repair of aorta for aortic aneurysm and aortic dissection (L18-L21, L27-L28)

When multiple segments of the aorta are replaced/repaired and the individual segments are classifiable to different four character codes, each segment replaced/repaired must be coded separately.

The replacement of the aortic arch must be classified to a code for the replacement of thoracic segment of the aorta, followed by **Z34.2 Aortic arch** to further specify the particular section of the thoracic aorta.

The replacement/repair of a juxtarenal abdominal aortic aneurysm/dissection has an increased level of surgical and postoperative complexity, and must be assigned the appropriate code for the replacement/ repair of a suprarenal aortic aneurysm/dissection.

The open replacement of the aorta for an aortic dissection without aneurysm must be classified to categories **L20 Other emergency bypass of segment of aorta** OR **L21 Other bypass of segment of aorta.**

When a Frozen Elephant Trunk (FET) procedure has been performed, this must be classified using the appropriate open replacement/repair code from categories **L18 – L21** and a supplementary code from **O20 Endovascular placement of stent graft.**

See also PGCS15: Emergency procedures.

A Frozen Elephant Trunk (FET) is a single-stage hybrid procedure, combining a conventional open approach with endovascular techniques to treat extensive aortic aneurysms or aortic dissections.

~~The repair of a juxtarenal abdominal aortic aneurysm would be coded to repair of suprarenal aortic aneurysm as these types of aneurysms have an increased level of surgical and postoperative complexity.~~

Chapter M Urinary

New guidance has been provided to differentiate between the OPCS-4 codes **M70.6 Radioactive seed implantation into prostate** and **M71.2 Implantation of radioactive substance into prostate**

Radioactive seed implantation into prostate (M70.6) involves the implantation of radioactive seeds into the prostate gland which are placed via hollow needles inserted through the skin. The needles are then removed while the seeds remain in place permanently, eventually becoming biologically inert.

Implantation of radioactive substance into prostate (M71.2) involves the insertion of a thin plastic tube(s) into the prostate gland. A radioactive source is then placed into each tube. After treatment is complete the tubes are removed, leaving no radioactive material in the prostate gland.

Chapter S Skin

PCSS1 has been updated to reflect the changes to **PCSZ2: Laterality of operation (Z94**)

PCSS1: Unspecified excision of skin lesion (S06.9)

Unspecified excision of skin lesion of any site other than the head or neck must be coded as follows:

> S06.9   **Unspecified other excision of lesion of skin**
> **Z site code**
> Z94.-   **Laterality of operation** (~~when skin of a paired organif applicable~~)

Example:

Primary suture of laceration of skin on the left side of the back

> **S42.1   Primary suture of skin NEC**
> **Z49.4   Skin of back**
> **Z94.3   Left sided operation**

Chapter V Bones and joints of skull and spine

Image control used for checking position of reduced fractures and the correct siting of fixators

See: PCSY7: Approach to organ under image control (Y53 and Y78).

- ~~*PGCS13: Image control used for checking position of reduced fractures and the correct siting of fixators*~~

PCSV5: Lumbar interbody fusion (V33.3, V33.6, V38.5 ~~and,~~ V38.6 <u>and V51.1</u>)

Chapter W Other bones and joints

PChSW2 has been updated to provided clarity on the use of **W84.8 Other specified therapeutic endoscopic operations on other joint structure.**

PChSW2: Arthroscopic procedures (W84.8)

~~If neither a specific endoscopic (arthroscopic) code nor a dedicated open code exists for a procedure performed arthroscopically then the following codes must be assigned:~~

> ~~**W84.8   Other specified therapeutic endoscopic operations on other joint structure**~~
> Z site code
> ~~**Z94.-   Laterality of operation**~~

For procedures performed arthroscopically, code **W84.8 Other specified therapeutic endoscopic operations on other joint structure** must only be assigned when:

- There is no specific 4th character endoscopic (arthroscopic) code that classifies the procedure
- There is no specific 4th character open code that classifies the procedure
- There is no **.8 Other specified** code in any other endoscopic or open category that describes the organ or structure on which the procedure is performed

See PGCS1: Endoscopic and minimal access operations that do not have a specific code.

PCSW12 has been updated to include an additional site code to add specificity to unspecified site osteotomy codes.

PCSW12: Osteotomy of the foot

When coding foot osteotomies, the appropriate OPCS-4 category will depend on the method of osteotomy and whether the osteotomy was performed on a single metatarsal, on multiple metatarsals, or on the phalanges.

There are <u>many</u> ~~a number of~~ codes within Chapters W and X that specifically describe different methods of osteotomy, e.g. angulation periarticular osteotomy (**W12.-**) or displacement osteotomy (**W13.2**); these terms must be documented in the patient's medical record and the appropriate index trail must be followed to assign these codes.

Osteotomies are often documented with the use of eponyms: however, the use of eponyms (e.g. Akin osteotomy, Scarf osteotomy) within clinical coding is discouraged. Where an eponym has been used by the responsible consultant and the specific type of osteotomy (e.g.'displacement', 'periarticular angulation' etc) has also been stated, rather than using the Alphabetical Index of Surgical Eponyms, the clinical coder must assign codes for the specific type of osteotomy using the Alphabetical Index of Interventions and Procedures.

See also PRule 8: Surgical eponyms

Osteotomies of the foot must be coded as follows:

Osteotomy/ osteotomies of multiple metatarsals of the same foot

All osteotomy/ osteotomies carried out on more than one metatarsal of the same foot must be assigned the following codes, regardless of the method used:

> **W03.2   Osteotomy of multiple metatarsals or W03.6 Osteotomy of multiple metatarsals and fixation HFQ**
> Z site code(s) (where this adds further information)
> **Z94.-   Laterality of operation**

PCSW12: *continued*

Osteotomy/ osteotomies of a single metatarsal, specified method

For osteotomy/ osteotomies of a single metatarsal, where the method of osteotomy is specified the following codes must be assigned. The OPCS-4 Alphabetical Index must be used to assign the appropriate osteotomy code:

W12.- Angulation periarticular division of bone or **W13.- Other periarticular division of bone** or **W14.- Diaphyseal division of bone** or **W77.5 Periarticular osteotomy for stabilisation of joint**
Z site code (where this adds further information)

W28.1 Application of internal fixation to bone NEC or **W30.1 Application of external fixation to bone NEC** (if fixation is used, and is not already implicit in the osteotomy code description)
Z site code (where this adds further information)

Z94.- Laterality of operation

Osteotomy/ osteotomies of a single metatarsal, unspecified method

Osteotomy/ osteotomies of a single metatarsal, where the method of the osteotomy/ osteotomies is not specified, must be coded as follows:

W15.- Division of bone of foot*
Z site code (where this adds further information)

W28.1 Application of internal fixation to bone NEC or **W30.1 Application of external fixation to bone NEC** (if fixation is used, and is not already implicit in the osteotomy code description).
Z site code (where this adds further information)

Z94.- Laterality of operation

*Code **W15.7 Osteotomy of bone of foot and fixation HFQ** must only be assigned when the metatarsal osteotomy cannot be classified to a site specific code in category **W15.-**. If a site specific code is available in category **W15.-**, use the site specific code with code **W28.1** or **W30.1**, a Z site code and **Z94.-**.

Osteotomy/ osteotomies of phalanx, specified method

For osteotomy/ osteotomies of a phalanx, where the method of osteotomy is specified the following codes must be assigned. The OPCS-4 Alphabetical Index must be used to assign the appropriate osteotomy code:

W12.- Angulation periarticular division of bone or **W13.- Other periarticular division of bone** or **W14.- Diaphyseal division of bone** or **W15.6 Cuneiform osteotomy of proximal phalanx with resection of head of first metatarsal** or **W77.5 Periarticular osteotomy for stabilisation of joint**
Z site code (where this adds further information)

W28.1 Application of internal fixation to bone NEC or **W30.1 Application of external fixation to bone NEC** (if fixation is used, and it is not already implicit in the osteotomy code description)
Z Site code (where this adds further information)

Z94.- Laterality of operation

> **PCSW12:** *continued*
>
> **Osteotomy of phalanx, other specified method or unspecified method**
>
> Where phalangeal osteotomy is performed and the method specified is not classifiable to one of the categories listed above, assign the following codes:
>
> **W15.7 Osteotomy of bone of foot and fixation HFQ** (if with fixation) or **W15.8 Other specified other division of bone** (if without fixation)
>
> Z site code (where this adds further information)
>
> **Z94.- Laterality of operation**

Example:

Closing wedge osteotomy of left proximal phalanx of the great toe, internal fixation with a screw.

W13.3	Cuneiform osteotomy NEC
<u>Z80.3</u>	<u>Phalanx of great toe</u>
W28.1	Application of internal fixation to bone NEC
Z80.3	Phalanx of great toe
Z94.3	Left sided operation

Chapter X Miscellaneous operations

Reference to the type of anaesthetic has been removed from **PCSX17**.

> **PCSX17: Anaesthetic without surgery (X59)**
>
> Codes in category **X59 Anaesthetic without surgery** are used to code patients who ~~receive a general or spinal anaesthetic~~ <u>are anaesthetised,</u> but who do not subsequently undergo the procedure they were anaesthetised for. The type of anaesthetic given may be coded in addition if this information is required to be collected locally. ***See PCSY10: Anaesthetic (Y80–Y84).***

The first example has been updated in **PCSX20** to reflect the accurate use of a radiotherapy body system code.

> **PCSX20: Radiotherapy (X65, X67–X68)**

Example:

Preparation and delivery of pulsed dose brachytherapy therapy for prostate cancer

X68.3	Preparation for interstitial brachytherapy
M71.2	Implantation of radioactive substance into prostate
X65.3	Delivery of a fraction of interstitial radiotherapy
	Note: Use a subsidiary code to identify introduction of radioactive material (Y35, Y36)
	Note: Use a subsidiary code to identify brachytherapy (Y89)
Y35.4	Introduction of radioactive substance into organ for brachytherapy NOC
Y89.2	Pulsed dose rate brachytherapy treatment
~~Z42.2~~	~~Prostate~~

Chapter Y Subsidiary classification of methods of operation

PCSY7 has been updated to incorporate the contents of, and expand on, the deleted standard **PGCS13**. Additional examples have been added to illustrate the correct use of the standard.

PCSY7: Approach to organ under image control (Y53 and Y78)

The following applies to codes in categoriesy **Y53 Approach to organ under image control and Y78 Arteriotomy approach to organ under image control:**

- When a procedure has been performed using image control and the code that classifies the procedure **does not** state the type of image control used, then a code from these categories **must be** assigned. If the specific method of image control is not stated, the fourth-character **.9** must be assigned

- The code(s) from categories **Y53** or **Y78** must be sequenced after the intervention and before the site and laterality codes

- If the code that classifies the procedure states the type of image control used, then a code from these categories **Y53 or Y78** *must not* be assigned. e.g. **L72.6 Intravascular ultrasound of artery NEC** and **Q51.1 Transvaginal ultrasound guided aspiration of ovarian cyst**

- If the type of image control used is implicit in the procedure, i.e. the procedure is always carried out using one specific form of image control, then a code from these categories **Y53 and Y78** *must not* be assigned: E e.g. **R37.3 Fetal biometry** which is always carried out using ultrasound.

- If image control has been used before, during or after a procedure as a method of checking the anatomical position, or the position of a prosthesis/fixator after insertion, or to confirm a procedure is complete, a code to classify the image control *must not* be assigned.

Y53 Approach to organ under image control

Codes in category **Y53 Approach to organ under image control** are used as additional codes for any procedure that uses image control that may or may not be performed via percutaneous approach. This excludes those procedures performed using an arteriotomy approach under image control (**Y78**).

- Where a number of different types of image control have been used together a code for each type of image control used must be assigned. The exception to this is fluoroscopy when used with an image intensifier, where it is only necessary to assign code **Y53.4 Approach to organ under fluoroscopic control**.

See also:

~~*PGCS13: Image control used for checking position of reduced fractures and the correct siting of fixators*~~
PCSY11: Gestational age (Y95).

Y78 Arteriotomy approach to organ under image control

Codes within category **Y78 Arteriotomy approach to organ under image control** must only be used where it is clear that an arteriotomy approach using image control has been performed. Common terms which indicate an arteriotomy has been performed are: incision into artery, surgical cut-down or cutting of artery.

The arteriotomy will always require closure with either suture or clips to the overlying skin and this must not be coded in addition.

The majority of interventions that are undertaken on arteries by radiologists and some surgeons are referred to as Interventional Radiology procedures and are minimally invasive. These are usually undertaken by putting local anaesthetic in the skin and then passing a small needle and tube into the artery without a surgical incision. This is referred to as a percutaneous access and the intervention is classed as a 'percutaneous transluminal' procedure.

Once inside the artery, the radiologist or surgeon needs a means of visualising the artery and this is achieved by using image control.

An arteriotomy is a method of approach used to gain access to the inside of the artery by surgical incision. Most patients having an arteriotomy will have a treatment that does not require image guidance as the surgeon will have a direct view of the artery. However, some interventions, in particular stent grafts for aneurysms, require incision away from the site of the procedure, and therefore require some form of image control to allow precise visualisation.

Examples:

Insertion of nasogastric feeding tube, ~~position of tube~~ into stomach,-, tube position checked with ultrasound to ensure correct siting ~~and positioned into stomach.~~

> **G47.8   Other specified intubation of stomach**

Open reduction of fragment of right scaphoid and screw fixation. The position of the screw was checked using image intensifier

> **W19.5   Primary open reduction of fragment of bone and fixation using screw**
> **Z72.2   Scaphoid bone**
> **Z94.2   Right sided operation**

L4/L5 posterior decompression for spinal stenosis, level checked with x-ray prior to incision

> **V25.5   Primary posterior decompression of lumbar spine**
> **V55.1   One level of spine**

Chapter Z Subsidiary classifications of site of operation

Reference to 'paired organs' has been removed from **PCSZ2** and guidance has been added.

PCSZ2: Laterality of operation (Z94)

When laterality is documented in the medical record, and is not already implicit in the code description, it must be coded. ~~Laterality must only be coded when coding procedures performed on paired organs.~~

~~Where it is necessary to assign more than one code to describe all the steps which took place during one procedure on the same anatomical site; the laterality code must only be assigned following all of the codes that are required to describe the procedure on the anatomical site.~~

~~Laterality must not be coded:~~

- ~~When the laterality is implicit in the code description~~

- When coding procedures on organs that are not paired~~.~~

PCSZ2: *continued*

When multiple procedures are carried out on the same site it is only necessary to assign the laterality code once after all of the procedures on that site, however there is nothing to prohibit the assignment of the laterality code multiple times in such instances, if a Trust has a local need to do so.

~~A 'paired organ' is one in which there are two separate organs of the same kind, usually one on either side of the body, for example lungs, eyes, testes, ears, arms, spinal nerve roots and teeth. Paired organs also include organs which are formed of definite lateral parts, for example the hemispheres of the brain and ventricles of the heart. Examples of organs which are not paired include pancreas, liver, rectum and trachea.~~